RAGNAR'S
TEN BEST
TRAPS

Bryce Lemmons

bandcalledlemmon
@ Yahoo.com

D G D G B-D
E A D G B e

RAGNAR'S TEN BEST TRAPS

And A Few Others That Are Damn Good, Too

Ragnar Benson

PALADIN PRESS
BOULDER, COLORADO

Also by Ragnar Benson:

Acquiring New ID
Do-It-Yourself Medicine
Eating Cheap
Guerrilla Gunsmithing
Live Off the Land in the City and Country
Mantrapping
Modern Survival Retreat
Modern Weapons Caching
Ragnar's Action Encyclopedia, Volumes 1 and 2
Ragnar's Guide to Interviews, Investigations, and Interrogations
Ragnar's Guide to the Underground Economy
Ragnar's Urban Survival
Survival Nurse
Survival Poaching
Survivalist's Medicine Chest
Switchblade: The Ace of Blades

Ragnar's Ten Best Traps:
And a Few Others that Are Damn Good, Too
by Ragnar Benson

Copyright © 1985 by Ragnar Benson

ISBN 0-87364-328-3
Printed in the United States of America

Published by Paladin Press, a division of
Paladin Enterprises, Inc.
Gunbarrel Tech Center
7077 Winchester Circle
Boulder, Colorado 80301 USA
+1.303.443.7250

Direct inquiries and/or orders to the above address.

PALADIN, PALADIN PRESS, and the "horse head" design
are trademarks belonging to Paladin Enterprises and
registered in the United States Patent and Trademark Office.

Visit our Web site at www.paladin-press.com

Contents

Introduction

Running a trap line is incredibly hard work. Yet for a lot of farm kids like myself raised in rural America during the Thirties and Forties, it was the only winter source of hard dollars.

My brothers and I had a line that eventually ended up being over ten miles long. It took at least one of us from right after we got done feeding the sows and filling the hay bunker in the morning till well after dark to look at every set. But if Dad had more work for us to do on the farm, we skipped some of the sets.

Dad was reasonable about our trapping, though. The fifteen or so dollars we made a week had an almost unbelievable impact on our total family well-being.

At first light, I would saddle up. Everybody has a different system. I carried a short three-quarter length Hudson Bay axe, a wading pole, and a four-peck pack basket. Instead of taking off my hip boots when I ran the line through the woods, I just left them on and turned them down. That way I didn't have to carry around the extra weight of my leather boots. It's a tough way to make a few bucks, but we didn't know of anything better in those days.

One particular day, I had been checking the trap line in and out of the creek and through the swamp and the woods since first light. After ten hours of foot-freezing trudging

An old, old picture of my brother and I with the first red fox I ever trapped. The pleasure was purely psychological, having outsmarted one of the area's really crafty critters. At the time, longhaired furs were not popular. I got $1.25 for the hide.

with a pack now filled with rats, a couple of coons, and an opossum, I was finally headed back to the house. It would be completely dark in about ten minutes.

It was the time of short-fur critters. Fox, skunk, and coyote didn't sell worth a damn. Beaver and muskrats did OK, but the real money-makers were mink. I hadn't, up to that time, ever personally caught one of the elusive brown critters. My brother had. Although I definitely knew how, I had never been lucky enough to nail a mink in one of my very own sets.

People in good physical condition used to hard physical labor develop a kind of reserve second wind. Late in the day with the end in sight, they actually pick up the pace. I've seen this myself many times: lumberjacks in Washington State, kids bucking hay in the withering sun in Illinois, horse wranglers in Wyoming, and Rhodesians on patrol on the Zambezi River. As I headed home, I picked up the pace, cutting across a shallow little creek that led past the north pasture field to our last line shack. The line shack was about a third of a mile from the big barn. Sometimes Dad or my brothers watched for me from the granary window as I came in at dusk. By today's standards, it was god-awful rough duty for a kid not even twelve years old.

A couple of days previous, I had made a set using an old, weak, leftover Number 1 long-spring trap under a big, old tilted flagstone. One of my brothers had brazed some nails on the trap for teeth. It sounds pretty makeshift, but at the time I thought it was first-rate. The water had washed away a big, dark tunnel under the rock. Ideal place for a bait set, I thought.

At the time, all I had left were a few bobwhite feathers and some sardine gravy in the bottom of one of those odd oval cans. I usually carried a few tins of cheap Norwegian sardines and either ate them for lunch or used them for bait. In this case, I did both.

Using a little stick for a scoop, I had dribbled the last of the gravy into the back of the hole. Then I threw in the quail feathers. The bait combination sounds as though I expected the mink to think a quail had caught and eaten a fish there.

Perhaps sixty meters from the set, I headed down the steep bank, intent on crossing the creek and walking to the flat stone in the water, where I had my little trap guarding the odd bait. I never made it.

A very heavy, ominous snakelike hiss stopped me cold in my tracks. It was a huge brown mink, caught by the front foot and madder than hell. The critter was so large, I later figured the only reason I still had him was because the trap had a drag and not a stake and because of the nail teeth.

Those were our prepistol days. As a result, because of the weight, I sometimes didn't carry a rifle. Unfortunately, this was one of those days. Under similar circumstances I would usually brain the critter with my axe, a good way to knock it out of the trap. Not something I was going to try this time.

So I ran for it. I ran more than a quarter of a mile to the cabin where I knew one of my brothers kept his Stevens Little Scout. One of my brothers saw me from the barn and knew something was up. He hollered to Dad.

Our barn where I lived during the summer when I was a kid. A small creek runs past the large cottonwood. We trapped the creek west to a river, then to a large bayou, and then through a hardwood forest back to the home place.

Running with the heavy pack nearly killed me. I threw it off at the shack, grabbed the little .22 single shot and three rounds of ammo, and headed back to the trap. My brothers and even Dad came running from the barn.

I stopped about twenty meters from the mink. It humped up defiantly and screamed. We used standard-velocity shorts to shoot game in traps. I drew a bead at its head, squeezed the trigger, and acquired my first mink.

About three weeks later, we sold it for $16.50, which I figured was just about all the money in the whole world. It was a time in my life when the best I could possibly hope for was $5.00 for working from 9:00 p.m. till 3:30 a.m. catching and loading chickens.

However, you won't find that famous old flagstone set among the traps I write about in this book. The best trap sets, in my opinion, are ones that consistently produce good results. As you will find out as you read this book, good results can be defined in a number of different ways. The important thing is that good results will replicate themselves again and again wherever the trap is used. It would be ridiculous for me to recommend that you go out and look for flat rocks under which to set home-modified steel traps. On the other hand, that old set is one that I still remember most vividly.

There is a tank trap that I used in southern Sudan which, like the flagstone set, I have a lot of nostalgia for. However, it can never be duplicated. In that regard, it isn't a particularly good trap for people to know about.

Other unique traps like these are the icebox set that I mention in *Survival Poaching* and the moose-snare trail set from *Live Off the Land in the City and Country*. If you want trap concepts and ideas, read these two books.

This manual is about little-known traps. Traps that are relatively easy to build and set and are consistent producers even when used in the far-flung corners of the world. Traps that are easy to maintain and will work on a variety of different animals. I have also included a chapter on baits. These are baits that are outstanding even in a worldwide context. Survivors and paramilitarists should know about them.

The following are my favorite traps, collected from over sixty years of experience in the bush. I hope you enjoy reading about them and have good success using them.

PART 1

The Ten Best

1. Bait

Good trappers know how to use bait. This includes not using bait when that's the best alternative as well as taking advantage of a situation where animals are attracted to a place, without actually using a baited set.

In this latter case, I am referring to the fact that in spring, deer will come to a salt lick and in the fall to an apple tree. Squirrels will travel miles to visit a ripe hickory nut tree, and bears will sell their souls for oats in the milk stage. The critters are attracted to an area and the trapper is smart enough to know why. It's a matter of identifying what is attracting the animals and then setting a trap that will catch the critter while its mind is on other things. This may sound simple, but many trappers I have met have never figured this part of the program out.

Bait, with a couple of notable exceptions, should be native to the area in which the trap is set. And don't mix up sets that should be baited with sets that are basically run sets. Run sets rely on the fact that game use a regular path.

Once when we were kids, I spotted a big old mink track along the river at a place where the water had washed under the bank. The water had eroded away all the soil, but left the sod layer on top. After a couple of months, the grass slumped down, breaking off at the new water's edge. A crack, perhaps sixty meters long and twenty-five centimeters deep, ran along the creek where the sod had split away from the high bank.

I saw the mink track after a spring flood swept the area clean. Later in fall, we decided to put a trap in the V-gully and see how it worked. My plan was to wade to the creek bank and carefully dig a clean, deodorized small trap in the crack. By placing a couple of sticks in the path, I hoped to get the critter to jump into the trap.

My brother thought we should put a small fish nearby on the bank to attract the critter. I thought that that would distract the mink. We got into a hell of a brouhaha about that set. Big brother was bigger, older, and had caught more mink than I, so I agreed. However, he didn't come when I made the set and I forgot the fish.

Four days later, the mink jumped into the trap with both front legs. It pulled itself, the trap, and the drag down to the creek and then drowned. It took maybe ten minutes to dredge it up with my Hudson Bay axe. This was not a bait set and never would be. At best, the mink would have ignored the fish. At worst, the fish might have alerted the critter. That old mink was using the path for reasons other than trying to find something to eat.

Good baits are usually the same thing the critter would like to find on its own roaming around the country. In the Midwest, fox, mink, and coons are suckers for a bit of pheasant guts hashed in with a bunch of feathers. Farther north, grouse guts work better. In the South, try quail.

If the critter is working an area for something like sweet corn, as in the case of fall coons, it usually works to take some of these kinds of groceries and move them closer to the animal's living area along with a trap or two. On the other hand, don't expect to buy an ear of corn in the Safeway and use it to bait coons in the middle of winter.

There are a couple of exceptions to this rule. Through the years, I have found that sardine oil left over in the can after you have lunched on the fish works fairly well on carnivores. Mink, coons, marten, fox, and skunk are some of the animals that will always come over to look if you put a teaspoon of sardine oil out for them. Another reasonably good, nonstandard bait is peanut butter and even better, honey.

Honey is, of course, native to a lot of areas in the U.S.

11

A lot of animals like it and will come after a properly presented honey bait. I found this out by accident quite a number of years ago when I spilled a few scraps of comb honey in a dying campfire. By morning, the critters had just about carried my whole firebox away.

The rule when using bait is either a whole lot or very, very little. A dead steer or horse, for instance, makes a wonderful bait for coyotes. However, ten handfuls of grouse feathers will just make them suspicious. It's best, in my opinion, to have the critter either search around for the bait or lose all fear because the bait is so overwhelming.

Bait won't make up for an otherwise sloppy set. If you don't know how to set a trap without leaving a scent or leaving the ground looking like you found it, the best bait in the world won't help.

Don't overlook the attraction of live bait. The Africans I worked with in Kenya and Somalia tied out goats to attract leopards. That worked OK, but a live dog worked far better. It was almost as if the leopard was in heat, it simply could not leave the dog alone.

In North America, I have used a live mouse—explained elsewhere in this book—a live chicken, and a live quail as bait. I have baited a trap by tying the bird's foot with a piece of string.

The set will attract critters easily enough, but getting them to put their foot in the trap is something else. Often they will come to the set, grab the bird, and make off with it without getting near the trap. Sometimes the bird has even gotten in my trap.

Down South, I have seen numerous otter and mink caught around live fish boxes. In the Midwest, a farmer's chicken house will eventually attract every weasel in the area even if the hens have been gone for years.

My success with scents has been mixed. This is true, I guess, because the relationship between attracting the critter and the scent is tenuous. One never really knows if that's why the critter showed up, or if it was for some other reason.

Besides that, it's tough to put the scent out without leaving human scent, thus undoing what you are trying to accomplish. I used to use an eye dropper, but most scent is too lumpy. Dipping a stick in the bottle leaves human smell from your fingers on the stick and isn't a viable alternative. The best, but not good, bet is to pour the scent on the set. It will not be properly mixed and you will use too much, but it's the only alternative.

I have had only limited success using artificial devices to attract furbearers. The one bad example that comes to mind is setting out a shiny piece of tinfoil in the hope that a curious coon will come over and step in the trap. I tried this set on and off for years and years and never caught a single coon.

Another idea that really has me puzzled is the wing-on-a-string gambit for bobcats. The idea is to hang a bird wing on a string from a tree limb so that passing cats will come over to inspect it and step in the trap. I have never got this idea to work, not even once. My brother has tried it in Canada and has had similar success.

Sometimes some pretty weird baits will work. In the western U.S. where I live now, coyotes are absolute suckers for house cats. I set them out live or dead with pretty similar results. Old tomcats especially will eventually attract every coyote in the region.

Still, my advice to the novice trapper is not to try and shortcut the procedure. Carefully look around to see what the carnivores are eating out in the wild. If possible, help a fellow trapper skin his catch. Check out the stomach contents to see what information you can pick up. Most of the time the critter's stomach will be empty. Now and then, however, you will hit pay dirt and pick up a valuable bit of information.

Another way of checking diets is to carefully look at animal droppings. Sometimes they will yield some good clues. Most trappers are probably like me, however; I have a hell of a time telling mouse hair from rabbit fur in coyote droppings.

Beyond these tricks, it's back to assessing the bird and mouse populations as well as looking for seasonal fruits, vegetables, and nuts.

2. Drain Tile Set

Farmers are replacing the old, traditional clay drain tiles that for so many years carried excess water off their fields with new plastic drain field pipes. Friends in the business who are shrewd about such things tell me that the switch makes economic sense and is probably the wave of the future.

Perhaps I am wrong, but I have never been able to catch the wide variety of animals at the entrance to a plastic drain that I can catch in the mouth of an old-fashioned clay type. It concerns me that the few farm boys who are left are going to be deprived of yet another opportunity to participate in what is a rapidly disappearing culture.

Through the years, I have caught a truly awesome array of different critters in the mouths of field drains. If the drain is running a bit of water into a creek or flowing ditch, usually you can find the traditional "Big Three": muskrat, mink, and coons. Yet I have managed to catch skunks, gray fox, opossums, nutria, barn rats, and even woodchucks and armadillos in wet tile sets.

Dry sets aren't as productive as tiles with some water flowing in them, but under some circumstances it is possible to catch most of the water critters as well as weasels, opossums, rabbits, squirrels, an occasional red fox, cats if there are any around, and even badgers.

Fox, raccoons, and muskrats, among others, are attracted to old drain tiles. Trappers can take advantage of this characteristic and really stack up on the pelts.

One of the best sets for badger I ever used was a variation of the drain tile set. We were running a line in north central Nevada into the Owyhee Mountains. This was only a few years back when prime Nevada coyote hides hit $110 and badger hides were $35. Mostly we ran a car line in the desert and the foothills. I kept it for about a month and a half till the snow got too heavy and I agreed to take another overseas job.

The badgers hadn't been trapped in that area for dozens of years, if ever. It was a good money-making plan while it lasted.

Readers who have run a line for badgers know that it isn't particularly difficult to get one to put its foot in a trap if they haven't gone into hibernation. The tough part is keeping them there. A badger can dig out forty fence posts in one night, if it sets its mind to it.

We solved part of the problem by putting a Number 3 jump trap in every road culvert we could find along our line. Instead of staking the trap, which I always think is a bad idea anyway, we used fairly large (75 cm. or so) chunks of angle or channel iron for drags. Most tile sets don't work a whole lot better with bait; road culverts in this situation were the exception. We baited with small handfuls of hashed-up jackrabbit and/or prairie chicken feathers and guts.

The results were dynamite. Every badger in the area seemed to want to stand in line to put its foot in our traps. The badgers didn't seem to care about the smell of steel around the metal culverts. Invariably, the trapped badger tried to escape into the culvert, but of course it couldn't dig through the pipe. Only one in five took off across the desert and even these guys didn't get far.

All of the traps were easy to check and rebait from our truck. And using a drag with a covered trap did not attract trap thieves, hawks, or eagles. About the only precaution we took was to check the traps on the more heavily traveled roads early in the morning. I am an early riser by nature, so often we ran the line from 4:00 a.m. till about 10:00 a.m. It was nice to be back at the barn by noon to start skinning the catch.

FRONT VIEW

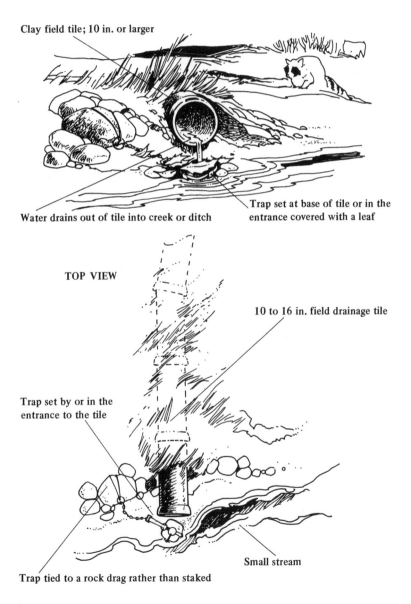

Clay field tile; 10 in. or larger

Water drains out of tile into creek or ditch

Trap set at base of tile or in the entrance covered with a leaf

TOP VIEW

10 to 16 in. field drainage tile

Trap set by or in the entrance to the tile

Small stream

Trap tied to a rock drag rather than staked

Drain tiles or, for that matter, road tiles work best when they are at least ten inches (25 cm.) or larger. Definitely the best combination is a twelve-inch (30 cm.) tile running back for a kilometer or two with a dribble of water flowing in it during trapping season. Running water kills the scent on the trap and attracts most animals. I realize that skunks, for instance, are not particularly enamored with getting their feet wet, but they will to get into a drain tile.

As kids on the farm, we trapped every tile in the country. One big sixteen-inch tile on the home place ran back four kilometers. One fall, a huge family of muskrats must have moved into the tile. My brothers and I got two per day the first six or eight days of the season. I ran the line the first day and made the original set. The second day I checked the trap, but all there was was a muskrat leg. Muskrats will frequently chew off their front leg—an occupational hazard of trapping muskrats in field tiles.

On a hunch, I checked the trap that afternoon coming in off the main line. There was a muskrat in the trap. My rifle was back at the house so I tried to brain the rat with my axe. That one got away, too. The rest of the week I checked the trap morning and evening, being careful to always have my rifle along. That's how we got so many muskrats in a row. From time to time, we picked up a coon. For that reason, I always used a Number 1 1/2 jump trap and a drag. The drag had to be long enough so the critter couldn't pull it back into the tile.

When setting the trap, be careful not to leave a lot of scent around the tile and also that the critter doesn't have to walk with its bare, sensitive feet across the trap spring and chain to get into the trap itself.

Don't make the set if it is impossible to use a drag and to cover the trap nicely. Drain tiles are only found in populated, well-settled areas. A trap thief who finds one of your sets will fold up your entire line by picking up every trap in every drain tile in the country.

3. Floating Duck Snare

Outside of a limited area in south central Ontario where the floating duck snare is extremely common, no one seems aware of its existence. I've not seen it any place in the eastern or western flyways, nor is it used in Mexico or South America to my knowledge.

Some twenty years ago, my older brother went to Ontario to work. It is frightening to remember how cavalierly we Bensons handled those kind of major relocations. As was the pattern in our family, he arrived on the scene virtually penniless with nothing more than a vague promise of a job. Usually, there wasn't even enough gas money left to move on if the job didn't come through. On the plus side, we all were confident of our ability to work long hours at hard labor and to live off the land on little or nothing if necessary.

Although we were generally pretty shrewd about taking game, it always seemed that wherever we went we learned a couple of often really remarkable new tricks from the local woodsmen.

I remember well going up to Fort Frances to see my brother after he had been there for a couple of months. My purpose was to see how he was doing. All my brother wanted to show me was the interesting trap the people in the area used to catch ducks.

Floating duck snares will work on any water where ducks land to feed. However, sheltered bays or shallow bayous where the snares can be checked in relative privacy are usually best.

This trapper set out several floating duck snares among his decoys. Note the two snared ducks tangled in the brush. The results were excellent.

Since that time I have used the set often. It works wherever grain-eating, aquatic birds sit on the water. I even showed it to some farmers living in northern Thailand. They used it to catch strange-looking chickenlike birds that live in the swamps in the area.

There are a lot of good things about the trap. It is simple, cheap, easily hidden from most people, effective, and will work as long as the water does not freeze. Sometimes, it will even work after the freeze. The principal disadvantage is that the floating traps will sometimes drift away from the trapping area and either become lost or ineffective. I don't like to lose traps of any kind. In the last twenty years, I have lost dozens of floating duck snares. They are not valuable; it's simply the principle involved.

Sometimes the traps can be put out using hip waders. Usually, it is best to figure on having some kind of a small boat with which to check the traps. If a boat is necessary to set the traps, the survivor faces another limitation. A lot of people simply don't have access to a boat.

Another serious defect relates to the fact that on fairly open water, floating snares are as obvious as cheap perfume to anyone who knows what to look for. My brother and I pulled in right behind the warden's truck one time that first summer I visited him. The warden was standing on the water's edge, binoculars in hand, looking for duck snares. We didn't have any out in that particular bay, but it taught us a valuable lesson regarding the proper method of setting the traps.

Floating duck snares can be made with just about anything that will hold up the bait and the snares. We have used old wood planks, wood blocks, and gallon jugs, among other things. All of these floats work. Yet the best and easiest to use is a 32-ounce or larger soda bottle. The modern plastic kind is just great.

Experiment with the bottle to determine how much gravel to put in it so that the bottle will float upright in a stable "seaworthy" position. The trick is to have as much neck as possible exposed out of the water, without allowing the bottle to tip over and float on its side. After ballasting the

Six strands of hair-thin copper wire
pulled from an old appliance cord
and made into snares.

Wheat, oats, or barley heads
tied to the bottle with straw

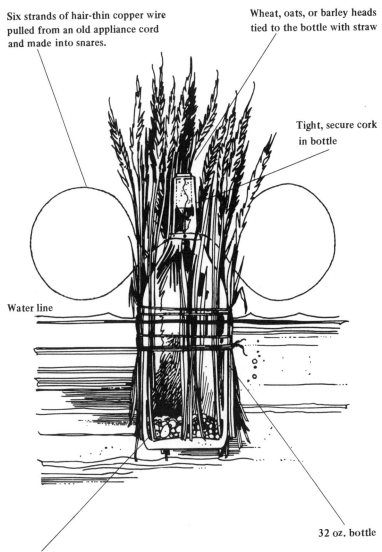

Tight, secure cork
in bottle

Water line

32 oz. bottle

Gravel ballast to keep bottle in an upright position

bottle, seal it up. Take care to do a proper job or the bottle will sink after an hour or two of being dragged around by a thrashing duck. The best method, in my opinion, is to cork the bottle and then cap it as well. Hot paraffin is a good material with which to seal the bottle.

Use whatever locally grown bait the ducks are used to eating. My brother still uses oats and barley. In Montana, I used wheat and rye. Peas work well, or even sorghum or corn if that's what the farmers in the area raise and the ducks eat.

The method by which the bait is fastened to the float is important. It relates to the form in which the bait is used. My daughter is a top-of-the-line kitchen manager. She claims that it isn't just the food, but the presentation, or how it looks when it comes out on the plate, that is equally important. I know it works on wild animals and I suppose it works on people as well.

It is certainly true when baiting traps. You have to make it look right. "Right" for a duck snare is to take the stalks of raw wheat, oats, rye, sorghum, or whatever and tie the grain, stalks, heads, and all on the bottle. I generally use baling twine. Bakery string or any other string will work just as well. The idea is to tie enough straw and grain on the bottle to make it look like a small floating shock of edible feed grains.

Mounting the snare comes last. Use six or eight strands of thin copper wire pulled from an electrical appliance cord. Each wire should be about 50 cm. long. This is enough to securely tie onto the neck of the bottle and still have sufficient length to fashion a six- to seven-cm. loop.

My brother feels he gets more ducks using three snares per bottle. I don't think it makes a damn bit of difference whether it is two or three. If there are ducks in the area, they will come over, feed on the grain, and get caught.

Depending on how long the duck is in the trap, there will be from 10 percent to 50 percent of them that will thrash around so much they will suffocate. My brother ties a small knot in the snare so that it can't close completely. This seems to help some.

I check my snares the second hour after daylight every day the snares are out. That way I limit the number of dead birds that end up in my bottle snares. Instead of automatically using the dead birds for bait in my fox and coyote sets, I cut their heads off and see how well they bleed. A lot of them are OK.

The best place for floating snares is in the small marshy potholes where the ducks come to feed and drink. I don't think the small amount of bait ever pulls them out of the sky. If, for some other reason, the ducks land within fifty meters of the bottles, they will take the bait. If they take the bait, they will catch themselves. Although the trap will work on all kinds and sizes of ducks, I have never caught a goose or loon in one.

A word of caution. It isn't necessary to set out very many of these little hummers. If the ducks are there, it's not much of a project to get a whole winter's supply in a week.

4.
"Board-Against-a-Chicken-House" Set

The title of this chapter is a concession to readers who think the names I give to various traps are too colorful and thus obscure. Also, I can't think of a more sexy name for the damn thing, so it's the "board-against-a-chicken-house" set.

However, those of you who don't have a chicken house need not despair. The set works in many different places besides the side of a chicken house. You will, however, need to have a large, long board. On that point I can't compromise.

The set first began its evolution when Dad asked me to trap some rats that were under the board pile. Every working farm has a board pile. It's a place where the odds and ends left from building projects are kept for the day a piece of something or other is needed to make repairs. Ours was on the east side of our big horse barn. I set several traps in the pile but found that I caught the most rats in the trap right next to the barn. I also got a couple of opossums and a weasel!

Not too long after that, Dad decided to do a construction job using the board pile rather than buying new. He took everything except one old plank about 40 cm. wide and 5 meters long. I set the board up against the barn on an angle to form a tunnel and caught a gray fox in it the very same

Sometimes the same barn used to store the traps is a good place to make a set, especially if it houses livestock or is used to store feed. Mice, rats, and sparrows are attracted to grain. Mink, skunks, fox, and coons, among others, come to get the pests and can be caught by the shrewd trapper.

Skunks are probably the most common furbearer taken in a board-against-a-chicken-house set. When we were kids, we tried everything to get the skunk out of the barnyard without creating an environmental wasteland. I can't ever remember being successful.

night. There is nothing like success to reinforce a good idea. In this case, it was an excellent idea that my brothers and I have been using for fifty years now.

Mom, when she saw the gray fox, suggested that I set the trap by the hen house. For several mornings there had been new fox tracks in the snow. She correctly reasoned that it wouldn't be long before the fox would be trying with a whole lot more determination to get in and nab some of her egg machines.

I had to use the tractor and a chain to drag the board over to the chicken house. Long oak planks were mighty heavy back in the good old days. That night I caught a red fox. In those days, a red fox skin brought about eight dollars. Well worth the effort. It wasn't till after World War II that the price of long-hair furs dropped so dramatically.

Apparently, the trap works because wild animals will risk coming into a barnyard or close to a set of outbuildings to get an easy meal. When they do, they will always keep out of sight as much as possible by creeping as near to a building as possible or, if one is available, through a tunnel next to the building. The board leaning up against a wall simply makes things convenient for the critters.

Traps should be set in about half an arm-length on either end of the lean-to. That way the traps are protected from snow and rain, domestic animals, and trap thieves. I don't believe that bait would make the set one bit more effective.

Generally, I use a Number 1 1/2 jump trap with a drag rather than a stake. These sets are excellent for coons and fox, both of which might best be caught with a larger trap. However, larger traps don't work well on weasel and mink, so I compromise with the 1 1/2. Using a drag rather than a stake mitigates the fact that the trap is a bit small. Be sure to cover the set carefully.

The board-against-a-chicken-house set works well in the city and in the really rugged back country. A few years ago, I caught a number of marten around an old cabin high in the mountains west of Libby, Montana. I set a trap behind a board leaning against the cabin wall. The snow got very deep, but under the cabin's eaves, sheltered by the big board, the

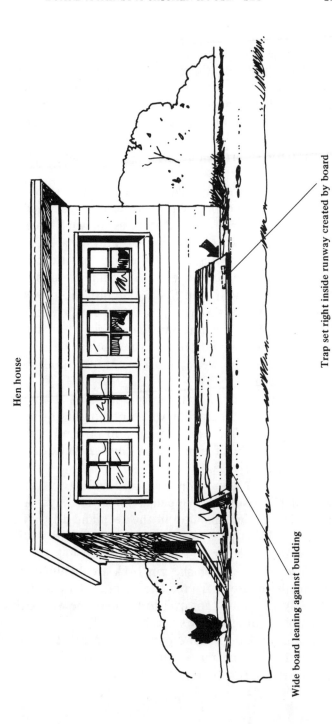

Hen house

Wide board leaning against building

Trap set right inside runway created by board

set kept on cranking out fur like a champ all winter long.

The other place the board set really works well is in the city. Using this set, it's possible to catch every rat and tomcat within a thousand meters without the neighbors ever knowing what's going on. A lot of medium-sized midwestern and southern cities have a sizable population of coons, opossums, squirrels, rabbits, and even some skunks. The set isn't real hot for squirrels but does very well on the rest of the list.

Lean the board up against a garage or house in a spot where flower beds or shrubbery can screen the animal's approach. A source of food such as an apple tree or small garden will help attract wild animals into the area.

The most interesting use of the trap that I can remember is the time my wife Kirsten nailed some marauding critters around her pheasant pen. She had about 250 pheasant in an enclosure that we thought was pretty much varmint-proof. It was fall, and the pheasants were a mature six to eight months old. We would put out three or four birds at a time for city dudes who were paying twenty-five dollars a day to hunt on our land.

Something started getting one or two birds a week, but we couldn't figure out what, or how it got in the pen. Since the birds flew, we had the top covered with chicken wire, and we didn't figure it was a chicken hawk or a fox that was jumping the wire.

Kirsten set a trap behind a board laid against the side of the bird pen. Nothing happened for a few days. About the fourth day, I saw her jump in the Jeep and drive over to the pen to feed her pheasants. I was chopping corn stalks in a field north of the pen.

A few minutes later she ran back to the Jeep and raced back to the house. I figured she had a critter and didn't have a gun. By the time I got over to the pen, she was back with a .22 pistol. Another red fox was history.

Two days later, she caught a huge old tomcat, which apparently was the real culprit. Before she could shoot, her Airedale ran over and crunched the cat.

5. Den Trap

Most, if not all, of the really good trapping skills I acquired when I was a kid came from my Uncle Dugan. Uncle Dugan was half Ojibway Indian. He married my mother's youngest sister and, in the total scheme of things, was not much older than I. As I remember, he was about twenty-six when I was nine.

By the time I was sixteen, Uncle Dugan was thirty-three and running one hell of a line of bear traps, among other things. Some of our experiences on that line trapping North America's largest furbearers would make an interesting book in and of itself.

One of the truly remarkable trapping systems that Dugan taught me was the common den trap. Fifty-some years later, having built and set up literally hundreds of them, I am still convinced that this one trap is absolutely the best there is in North America. No other trap comes even halfway close to doing what the den trap can do.

On one memorable occasion, my youngest brother caught five skunks at one time in one. Another time he got four. A few days later he got three raccoons. This says nothing about the huge number of rabbits, squirrels, opossums, muskrat, mink, weasel, red and especially gray fox, and coyotes we have picked up through the years. We have even caught quail, pheasant, and snakes in den traps.

Virtually every animal in North America that lives on land will go into a hole in the ground and can be taken in a den trap. I have from time to time cornered a coyote in my artificial dens, although it is not common because I generally build the entrance to the den too small.

My brother lives in a remote area of Ontario where the right to a trapping territory is assigned by the provincial government. Because these assignments preclude all but an elite few from trapping in the area, my brother has had to resort to other techniques. One of the principal and best tools at his disposal is the den trap.

A den trap will work at all times of the year. It requires no bait and is completely undiscoverable from even the sharpest woodsman. I have never had one of my den traps

Sometimes it is possible to catch two or three critters at once in a den trap. If their pelts are not in demand or the critter is small, the animals can be released unharmed.

discovered, but my brother told me recently of the closest he ever came to having it happen. One of the concession-holders whose territory he traps actually tracked a fox to the den. The guy set a conventional steep trap in the den entrance!

Through the years, my brother has caught an incredibly diverse number of critters in his line of den traps. I have the first fisher he ever caught in a den trap, and incidentally the first fisher I ever saw, hanging on the wall of my den. It's a big, old male that at the time had relatively little value because of its coarse fur.

About the only animals we have never caught in a den trap are bobcat, otter, and badger. I set a line out a few years back in northern Florida near the town of Hastings. We got a lot of opossums, coons, and gray fox as well as an occasional armadillo. A close friend later set some den traps in southern Georgia and got a number of nutrias.

Cost for the raw materials to build a den trap is about the same or a little more than the retail price of a Number 3 jump trap. This does not include the initial labor required to build the trap, which can also be significant. After the traps are built, it will take a day of hard labor to set out two under the very best of circumstances. When we were kids, we figured we were doing good to get one out in a very long day. And this was just installing or "setting" the trap. My brothers and I built them in the barn during the winter when nothing much else was happening.

The trap should be located in an area where game travels or lives. Put it on a gentle slope along a game trail, near a spring or creek, or at the corner of a field in a thicket. I have even set them up in the middle of town in a lilac hedge.

By the time I was sixteen, we had one in every woodlot within five miles of our home in the Midwest. It didn't matter if we checked the trap once a week or once a month. The critters were always waiting when we got there, safe and sound, out of harm's way.

The heart of the trap is an artificial den constructed of sound lumber, buried from 25 to 35 cm. under the ground. Make the box out of the best rot-resistant lumber you can find. Cyprus is best, but seldom available anymore. Another

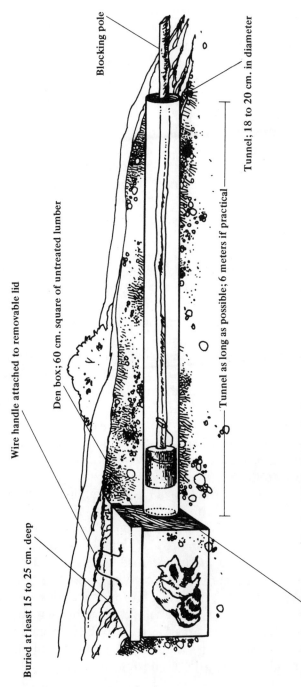

Blocking pole

Tunnel; 18 to 20 cm. in diameter

Tunnel as long as possible; 6 meters if practical

Den box; 60 cm. square of untreated lumber

Wire handle attached to removable lid

Buried at least 15 to 25 cm. deep

Tunnel enters den box a couple of centimeters above the floor.

good material is rough-cut cedar. Oak planking or three-quarter-inch marine plywood also works. The worst material—which I have occasionally used because it was all there was available—is 2.5 cm. pine. Traps built of pine will usually only last a couple of years. Animals will not generally use den traps made of wood that has been painted or treated with wood preservatives.

Construct the den box so that it ends up a 60- to 70-cm. square. Build it as soundly and as tightly as possible. Drilling a few one-cm. holes in the bottom helps if the area is damp. Do not plan to set the den out in a place where it might get flooded. Den traps work well along creeks if the tunnel slopes down to the water's edge and the box is buried in the bank above the waterline.

Leave the top of the box open and construct a tight lid. Put a lip on it so that the lid centers on the box. To be effective, the lid must keep out water and light. Sometimes I put a piece of tar paper or galvanized tin on the top to protect it. A piece of dog chain or Number 9 wire works well as a handle on the box lid.

Next, built or scrounge together material for the tunnel. I have used old iron pipe, secondhand culverts, clay tile, and even four boards nailed together in a square. The tunnel should be 18 to 20 cm. on a side although I have used tunnels as small as 15 cm. Everything but plastic pipe seems to work well as tunnel material. Most wild animals don't seem to like to crawl up plastic pipe. Too bad! It sure is light and easy to carry into the woods.

The length of the tunnel has a dramatic impact on the performance of the trap. Anything less than two meters simply will not work. Six meters is ideal but usually impractical. Usually, the trapper has to carry the trap into the set on foot. The box and lid make one load for sure, and maybe two. Three or four more packs carrying tunnel sections into the trap location are generally a bit too much. I usually settle for four meters, unless I have an old piece of lightweight aluminum culvert or can carry the stuff to the trap site in a truck.

After building or scrounging together the tunnel, cut out the tunnel opening in the lower corner of the den box. Be sure to put the entrance hole at the lower corner—not in the middle and not up off the bottom. The critters tend to fill the box with trash if the opening is above the floor of the box.

Take special care to cut out the opening slightly smaller than the tunnel. Later, you will push a block up the tunnel with a pole. The block should not end up in the den. You want it to hit on the den box entrance and stop, closing off the entrance.

Bury the box and tunnel at a prescouted, preselected location. Be sure the entrance to the tunnel surfaces at least five centimeters below the ground, and that the tunnel body is nicely covered with earth. The object is to both hide the trap and keep light from entering anywhere but the tunnel entrance.

The entrance must not be obstructed so that the blocking pole can be easily slid up into the tunnel. Nearby trees and brush become a nuisance if the planning phase of this operation is initially weak.

In fall and winter when I am looking at the trap weekly, I will sometimes cover the trap lid with duff. During spring and summer, I bury it with a good, solid layer of dirt. All this depends on the local conditions, how often the trap will be checked, and how much it has to be camouflaged.

A trap buried in spring will attract some critters by winter. Usually it works much better if it has been in place for at least a year. I have had some den traps work well for ten years or more, with little or no repair.

Cut a blocking pole for each set and leave it by the trap, leaning against a tree or lying in the brush. The block itself can be carried along if the tunnels are all about the same size. It's too much work to carry the pole around from trap to trap in the woods.

Drill a hole in the block and whittle one end of the pole down so it is a good pressure fit. I also tie the block to the pole with a piece of wire so it won't loosen in the hole.

About once a week during the trapping season, approach the trap quietly from down tunnel and, using the pole and block, close off the entrance to the den. Pull the lid up and look inside the den. Even a fierce coon or mink will cower in the den for a few moments, giving you a good chance to get off a shot with a .22.

Except for multiple skunks, I have never had a critter jump out of the trap. In the case of the skunks, I had to momentarily retreat after the first shot, allowing some of them to jump out. They were easy to shoot on the ground around the trap.

Blood and animal scent around the trap does not seem to make a bit of difference. Often I have picked up critters two days in a row.

Like most good traps, the den trap is a model of simplicity. Anyone I know of who has tried one has been more than pleased.

6. Live-Mouse Set

Readers who have a copy of *Live Off the Land* will recognize this trap. It was somewhat the centerpiece of the book—my offering to readers who wanted a dynamite trap that they wouldn't likely hear about except in one of my books. Since this book is about really good, effective traps and at least four of my books allude to trapping, there is bound to be some overlap.

Trappers who have tried the set and taken the time to write to me agree with my assessment that there is virtually no set that will do better on coyotes, fox, bobcats, and badgers. On the down side, readers who have tried the trap for the first time suggest that I haven't gone into enough detail explaining how the trap works.

Basically, the idea is to set out a live mouse as bait for mouse-eating critters. Of course, the set must be in a place where mice are likely to live and where coyote-bobcat-fox-type predators are likely to visit. It also takes a bit of intuition to know how to put in the set so that the animal is not so puzzled it immediately starts looking for the trap.

Given all of this, the toughest part of the operation is often related to catching a live mouse and then keeping it alive. There are several methods of accomplishing this mouse-catching business. It's possible to turn over an old log or board and find a colony of mice. Farmers with granaries can

Bobcats are great mousers. In winter, mice are often all they will get to eat for weeks on end. A good live-mouse set will clean up most bobcats within three to four kilometers over the course of one winter.

Badgers will come to a mouse set. If they are common in your area, use a big enough trap.

catch mice that have fallen inside, or you can set out a trap that catches live mice. Almost any small-town hardware store will have such a trap. They are made out of galvanized sheet metal and hardware cloth, about 12-cm. square, and cost in the eight- to ten-dollar range.

The trap works on a windup principle. It is wound like an alarm clock. The mouse runs down the tunnel looking for the wheat grains, flour, or cheese bait and hits the spring-wound trigger. When tripped, the trap sweeps the live mouse into a holding compartment and resets itself. About eight or nine mice can be caught before the trap has to be rewound.

Live, wild mice are easily traumatized. It is best not to try to handle them or they will almost certainly scare themselves to death. I run the mice into a small cheesecloth butterflylike net to remove them from the trap. From the net, they will usually move right into the holding bottle without too much problem.

Use an old apple-juice bottle to house the mouse. Virtually any bottle having a sound screw lid will work. However, big gallon jugs are tough to dig into the set and hide, and little mayonnaise jars don't provide much living space for the mouse. Before putting the mouse in the jar, fill it half full with leaves, straw, or grass and a couple handfuls of grain. Punch a number of small breathing holes in the lid. It is also helpful to cover the jar with cloth or paper so the mouse doesn't become frightened looking out the glass when you carry it around.

I put the mouse in the bottle and then wait several days to be sure it will live. It isn't uncommon for mice to die after a day or two. Mice, for those who wondered, get enough moisture out of raw grain to live on for several months. It isn't necessary to put water in the bottle.

The best location for the set is under an old stump on a slightly sloping hill, facing a grassy patch in fairly extensive woods. Old stumps are where mice hang out naturally. That location is also protected a bit from snow and rain. The dry rotting wood is ideal to cover the trap. Heavy brush surrounding the set will give the animals a sense of security as they approach. The grassy area is a place where predators play around anyway, looking for mice.

Don't locate the bottle in a place where it is so wet, the bottle will freeze in solid. On the other hand, the set works well along small creeks or ditch banks if one gives some thought to the cold, damp conditions that are often present.

Dig the bottle back into the slope or bank, taking care to handle the set the same way you would treat a dirt-hole set. Keep the human scent down as much as possible. Work from an old piece of deer hide or tarp. Carry off the excess dirt and don't smoke or spit.

Put the bottle in far enough so that the entrance can be lightly but thoroughly covered with a mixture of dirt, dry grass, and leaves. Finish the set by leaving a small dug-in looking spot with a light dirt spill over the trap.

Because of the many coyotes where I currently live, I use a Number 2 jump trap. If I were after nothing bigger than a mink, coon, or skunk, I would use a Number 1 1/2 jump

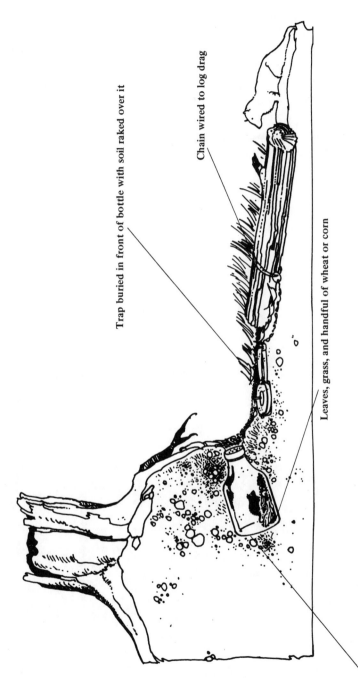

Trap buried in front of bottle with soil raked over it

Chain wired to log drag

Leaves, grass, and handful of wheat or corn

Mouse in bottle buried in a dry area beneath an old stump

trap. As is my custom, I fasten the trap to a log drag with a long piece of Number 16 wire doubled over twice for added strength. Once in the set, the mouse will usually last a month or two, on through the end of trapping season. Sometimes a caught badger or coyote will dig the bottle out. It doesn't happen very often using a drag.

The set is simple to make. Rather than further extolling its virtues, I suggest putting one in for a trial. I'll bet next fur season you will put in a lot more.

7. Chinese-Chopper Trap

Any book on favorite traps that I am involved with has got to include at least one mantrap. Mantraps, as readers of my book on this subject know, really interest me. I find the culture and people who develop these kinds of devices to be immensely interesting and the traps themselves to be the ultimate challenge. Man, after all, is the hardest quarry there is because of his collection of five senses, plus his intelligence.

Men do not usually have a highly developed sense of smell, and their hearing and sight are not as good as that of some animals. But taken altogether and coupled with a doubly better intelligence than any animal, one is dealing with a formidable quarry.

City-born-and-bred humans can't, of course, compete with people living out in the hills when it comes to staying out of traps. On the other hand, people from primitive societies don't do very well in towns. If nothing else, there is a strong propensity for them to get run over by taxis.

In the late Sixties, I was involved in a project that included bringing an incredibly skilled Somali tracker to town for the first time. Gaydu was about fifty years old and had lived in the headwaters region of the Giuba River all his life. He had never even been to one of the modest little towns in the region. Most of the people in his village had never seen a

European, and none of them had ever seen a white woman till my wife came along.

Gaydu was very skilled. He could track a single antelope in a herd of seventy-five for hours on end. I was with him when he followed a small party of humans for three days. I only saw three or four tracks the entire time, but this old bird never got off the trail.

We took him with us to Mogadishu, the capital of Somalia, and billeted him in a small house in a residential area. It wasn't residential Denver, but it wasn't grass huts, either. Americans, however, would not have recognized it as a single-family residential neighborhood. The street was unpaved. There was no water and no sewer. Various tropical trees and shrubs grew at random around the place which, as it turned out, was a good thing.

To Gaydu, all of the houses looked the same. Downtown, where the shops and the market were located, was obviously a blur of sameness. This absolutely incredible machine that could march fifty kilometers a day through the flat desert without ever getting lost could not get around the block without losing his way.

I have a vivid mental picture of him walking backward away from the house memorizing every tree along the street in an attempt to keep from getting lost. He was continually backing into a street or crossing anywhere at random, much to the consternation of those driving vehicles in the area.

Allah must have smiled on the old gent because we got him back to the bush safely without destroying his bush skills. He was an excellent example of a man who would be very difficult to trap, unless he came to the city. Then he would have been duck soup.

The principal reason I like the Chinese chopper trap is because it's a mantrap that I personally have set and actually seen work. In fact, a chopper I helped build performed an extraordinary miracle by working twice.

I was staying near the small town of Gatab at about the 1800-meter level on Mount Kulal in the Northern Frontier District of Kenya. During the late Sixties when I was there, Somali Shifta were raiding the region with such impunity

Most of the tribesmen I worked with at Gatab were Turkana, but there were also Rendille and Samburu on Mount Kulal. They were more solitary in nature and worried that my trapping abilities might anger the raiders.

that the district commissioner closed the area.

After Gatab was hit by raiders, we set out several traps along the mountain trails leading into the region as an almost stopgap protective measure. Eventually, the government sent thirteen police, but for the time we were on our own.

Mantraps are not as effective as booby traps, and they almost never have any real impact on the outcome of strictly military operations. They can, however, be built out of virtually nothing, using the most basic tools, and they can have a huge impact on the psyche of small units operating in the area.

Mantraps used against primitive people who are accustomed to observing things around them must be incredibly clever. When it comes to picking just the right spot where the trap is likely to blend naturally into its surroundings, pictures and words are never adequate. Like so many other things in this world, finding a good spot to place a successful mantrap is an art and not a science.

We found one of these locations at a spot about the 1800-meter level on a path that crossed a mountain saddle through a cedar thicket. Brush partly obscured the path. There were enough large trees to rig to, and the trail skirted along a steep rock canyon at that point. People traveling through the area were naturally funneled to the set.

We put the trap in, hoping we could catch some of the Somalis that we knew were in the area. Eventually, we did get two Rendille warriors. Through the grapevine, we also learned that at least one Somali had jumped off the cliff to avoid the trap but, remarkably, was not badly hurt. The Somalis are incredibly more alert than any of the Bantu, but to be able to jump off the trail down a very steep bank at night was beyond my comprehension.

The killing part of this trap is a piece of log about 2.5 to 3.5 meters long. A longer log is better if it doesn't become clumsy and if the density can be maintained. As a practical matter, it's tough to hoist, hold, and trigger a weight much more than 400 kg. An alternative is to hang a lighter log higher in a tree. That situation is tougher to find in the field. Also, a log dropping from six meters is easier to see and dodge than one dropping from four meters.

A good compromise is to cover one-half of a dry, light log—if that's all that is available—with twenty penny nails or even ten-cm. wooden pegs. The log from below should look like a prickly earth packer.

Start installing the trap by bringing the drop log to the trap site and suspending it from the tree limb a couple of centimeters off the ground. Position the rope so that the log hangs exactly parallel to the ground. Most places out in the field are not flat. Thus, the log will be tipped a bit one way or another to maintain its parallel position relative to the ground. After setting the balance, hoist the log up to its set position.

Sometimes the most difficult problem is screening the log from view. Unless it is really dark, people are just not going to walk under a big log covered with spikes hanging by a rope. The screen of brush or whatever can't be too thick. It seems incredible but small brush will sometimes partially deflect a huge, heavy log.

Triggers are tough for this kind of trap. The best is a trip

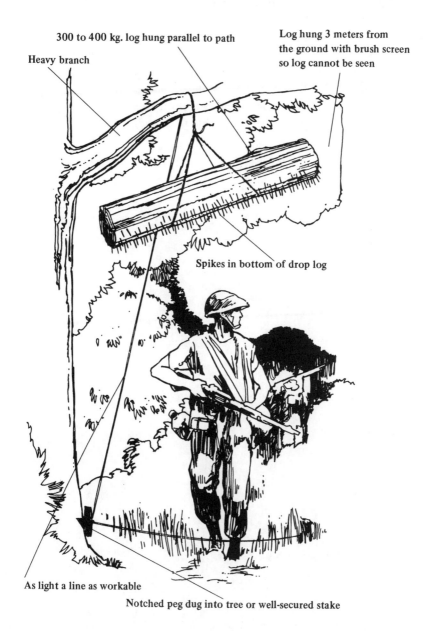

300 to 400 kg. log hung parallel to path

Heavy branch

Log hung 3 meters from the ground with brush screen so log cannot be seen

Spikes in bottom of drop log

As light a line as workable

Notched peg dug into tree or well-secured stake

peg. They can be made to take the weight and can be hidden. It is advisable to use a small live tree cut off about 25 cm. high and notched. If a tree is not available, drive a long and stout stake into the ground. One that is knarled or has stubs or branches on it, driven in backward, will best resist pulling.

No matter which trigger is used, it must be as short and light as possible. Otherwise it will be too slow and noisy to catch wily bush people

There are other good mantraps, but this one should do for those who have an urge to dabble with such things.

8. Rock Weir Fish Trap

In my opinion, the best place to look for a meal when in a suddenly traumatic survival context is any stream, river, or lake close at hand. Of course, bodies of water are not always the most logical source of food, even if one lives near the ocean. But the general concept continues to be a damn good rule of thumb with which to operate.

Bodies of water attract ducks and geese that come from great distances as well as aquatic animals such as muskrats that will make a pond their permanent home. Bodies of water are also likely to contain crayfish, cattails, and lily pads, all of which are not only edible, but are a delicacy.

Survivors, however, usually have the best luck going after fish. That's one of the reasons most survival packages contain a few fish hooks and some line. Catching fish with a hook and line is OK, yet not all that good, either. Waiting around to catch a few is often a hopeless waste of precious time.

There are a lot of traps that do a good job of catching fish. Few do as well or better than the rock weir trap. The good part about a rock weir is that it can be set in almost any creek or small river without tools and without any previously collected survival supplies. If you are in a light plane crash in the mountains, for instance, a rock or log weir can be put together with nothing more than human energy and initiative.

An ideal stream for a rock weir has lots of movable, large rocks close to a broad, open stretch of water from 25 to 35 cm. deep.

These trout and Kokanee were caught in the fall in a small rock weir upstream about three kilometers from a large Montana reservoir. The trout appeared to have gotten into the trap going downstream while the Kokanee were migrating upstream. Apparently, the trout jumped the last wall upstream to get in the trap.

The trap is truly a trap. Once built, no one has to sit and watch it, or otherwise tend to it. No bait is required, although baited weirs sometimes work better.

The most difficult part of operating a rock weir, assuming one has the energy to build the trap, is getting the fish out of the holding pens once they get inside. Sometimes the trapped fish swim around at unbelievable speeds and jump fairly high rock barriers when they know they are cornered. I have a couple of suggestions that will minimize this problem as well.

The best, most productive rock weir I ever put in was outside of Rapid City, South Dakota, downstream a kilometer or so from a state fish hatchery. I got the idea for the trap while working in Alaska during the early Sixties. Native fishermen used the devices to catch migrating salmon. They worked well, after a bit of modification, for smaller grayling as well.

The trap in the Dakotas took two of us two days to put in. The stream was about mid-calf deep at the place where we built the trap and perhaps twenty-five meters wide. We carefully planned the trap to make use of a number of large natural rocks and an island. Even so, the water was so deep, we soon ran out of nearby portable rocks. The only thing that saved us was the fact that several bunches of tourists and picnickers thought our project looked like fun. About twelve or fifteen of them put in about three hours each carrying rocks!

Eventually we got some really huge trout in the trap. The last pen was mostly very shallow, but some of these lunkers still managed to jump the rocks and escape.

Before starting, it is important to survey the creek or stream on which you intend to build the weir. Put the trap in where it will naturally fit with the least amount of work.

The general concept is to construct a barrier with small openings through which the fish can swim, either rock walls or, in mud-bottom rivers, a stake fence. As a general rule, these traps will produce more fish if they are located upstream from a large deep hole.

Lay out the walls so that they form a slight V-shape going upstream. The openings should be at the top of the V. Usually even nonmigratory fish such as catfish and carp will enter more easily going upstream. A slight V-shape makes it tougher for the fish to find their way back out of the trap when you go out to make the daily collection.

The openings should be on alternate sides of the creek if at all possible. They have to be located in a place where at least a small current flows so that the water is deep enough for the fish to swim. It isn't always possible to set the openings so the fish have to zigzag from one side of the creek to the other to get in the trap, but it certainly is desirable.

Try to avoid the situation where the trapped fish will have enough deep water in the last pen to get up a head of steam and race straight back through two or three openings out to freedom.

The last rock wall is just that. A rock wall, solid with no openings. Water must, of course, be able to run through the spaces between the rocks but there should be no openings large enough for fish. This last wall is the final barrier for the fish coming upstream into the trap. It is what holds them till the survivor arrives on the scene. The barrier wall is also what determines the size of the fish the trap will catch.

Water in front of wall must be shallow or the fish will jump the trap.

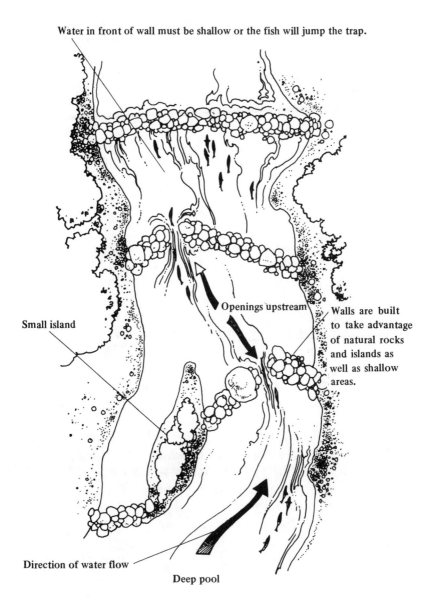

Small island

Openings upstream

Walls are built to take advantage of natural rocks and islands as well as shallow areas.

Direction of water flow

Deep pool

Wood stakes can substitute for rocks if rocks are not available or the creek bottom is muddy.

Very small fish will slip through the space between the rocks and continue upstream. There is little that can be done about this as long as the stream is flowing at all. A tight rock wall will become a dam. Trapped fish will simply find a low spot in the dam and slither over it upstream.

A spear is handy for getting fish out of the trap. In a survival situation, use a forked stick and either pin the fish or flip them out of the water.

Another method is to use a pair of pants as a kind of purse seine over the entrance to the last pool. Tie the pant legs off at the bottom and simply cover the opening in the rocks with the waist. If no one is standing at the opening, the fish will race right into the pants where they can be caught. A T-shirt will also work as a purse seine if the fish are not too large.

One of the best uses of the trap is to walk upstream and chase the fish ahead into the weir. Another method is to leave the trap overnight when the fish are migrating.

A variation of this trap works very, very well in tidal flats in the ocean. The number of fish that can be caught in one of these traps, set where a small stream runs into the ocean or in a shallow estuary, can be truly phenomenal—far more than one could eat. The fish come in with high tide, but can't leave when the water does.

It may also improve the trap to put some bait in the last pool. A couple of cans of dog food punched a few times will work. Deer guts are also OK. The best scheme for trout is to hang a large dead animal such as a porcupine over the creek. After a few days, the maggots will hatch and fall off into the water, attracting huge numbers of fish.

Lots of quick, easy food is available for the survivor who masters the use of this trap. All it takes is the will to make it work.

9. "Havahart" Traps

Recently, the first Havahart trap I ever bought bit the dust. I set it for a critter that I suspect was a big old coon, out under the deck in back of the house. Some animal had been coming in and getting the dogs' food, and making a mess out of our garbage can. Whatever it was got in my poor old worn out Havahart trap and just tore the hell out of it.

I originally bought the trap in the fall of 1954 to use to catch gray and fox squirrels. As I remember, it cost about $7.50 including shipping. In those days that was a lot of money, but the outfit has been worth the price many times over.

I estimate I have caught a minimum of 350 squirrels as well as innumerable coons, opossums, cats, muskrats, woodchucks, skunks, and even a few mink and fox in the trap. It worked so well because the trap is very simple, well designed, and extremely well made.

Animals entering a box trap like to be able to look out the other end, rather than seeing a blank wall. I believe that under the right circumstances they are even attracted to a trap that looks like a tunnel. Havahart traps open on both ends. However, the doors are controlled by a very sensitive, simple pan in the middle of the trap. All an animal need do is smell the pan and bang, the doors fall down and lock.

I have used Havahart traps for well over thirty years. Shortly before I finished this book, the original trap I bought for $7.50 in 1954 bit the dust.

Havahart traps come in many sizes from small rat to large dog. Currently, I use three different sizes, but for years I got along nicely with the size shown in the middle of the stack.

The trigger in the Havahart is simplicity itself. All the animal need do is touch the central pan and the ends drop down.

Camouflage of Havahart traps is more difficult than most traps but obviously not impossible as this picture of a set trap demonstrates. The winter brush is sparse, but the trap is not immediately obvious.

Havahart traps are set with both ends open. Animals are not nearly as suspicious when they can see through an enclosure. When the hinged doors drop, the wire locks are set in place.

The problem with my old trap was that through the years, various critters had weakened the door hinges until finally an especially big and powerful animal simply ripped the whole thing apart. That old war horse didn't owe me a thing. I was truly sorry to see it go.

Woodstream Corporation in Lititz, Pennsylvania, still makes Havahart traps. I don't think they are too popular because no hardware stores in my neck of the woods carry them. That's a shame because that trap is a damn good one. I called the company and it sent out a replacement. Prices are up considerably, but the same good construction prevails throughout. There are even some improvements like a carrying handle and an easier-to-use bait pan.

Havahart traps are box-type live traps, made of heavy gauge galvanized tin and hardware cloth. They come in a number of sizes from little rat or mink traps to ones that might catch a dog or coyote. There are two ways to set them, depending on the nature of the animals in the area and on the season. The trap can either be baited, set in a board pile, or set in a run alongside a barn at the entrance to a den. When the critter hits the pan, the ends fall down and are locked by a couple of sliding bars. If you are interested in trapping live critters, the Havahart is your trap. I suspect that the various fish and game departments use lots of them.

Wild animals left for any length of time in a Havahart will start to beat themselves up and bloody their mouths chewing on the wire. In that regard, the trap does not catch them completely unharmed. Domestic animals just sit in the trap and wait.

There are a couple of minor problems with Havahart traps. For one, it's pretty tough to afford enough traps to set out a line, and second, it's virtually impossible to carry the traps around to get out a line. They're just too big and heavy. I won't even put out a valuable Havahart away from the house in the woods where someone could nab it.

Another problem relates to the noise the critters make slamming around in the trap when they get caught. Even normally laid-back animals like skunks and opossums run around hammering the pan, and making all kinds of racket that will attract attention.

People who have not used Havahart traps generally perceive a third problem that generally does not occur. Havahart traps are not all that difficult to camouflage and hide. Set along the side of a building in a run under a bush, they are generally quite obscured. I have used my trap many, many times in the center of the city to pick up visiting animals without them ever being noticed.

Setting the larger traps can be a pain. The traps are so long that even a person with very long arms can't reach in and set the bait on the pan. It would be helpful if the maker put a small door in the center of the trap, but this is only a minor criticism.

The only other suggestion is that sometimes it helps to put a small amount of weight on the ends of the doors to make them fall faster. I use some medium-sized stones that roll

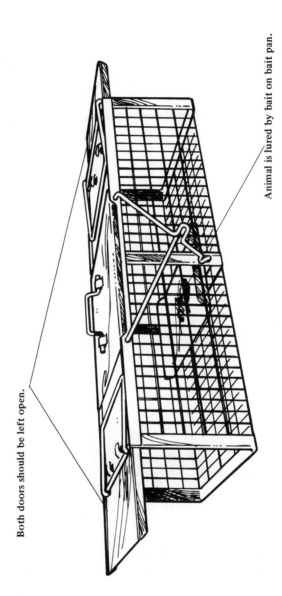

Animal is lured by bait on bait pan.

Both doors should be left open.

off when the trigger operates. So far, I haven't had a miss with this technique.

Animals in towns or built-up rural areas don't seem to mind the smell or look of the steel-galvanized trap. I have caught an animal a night for weeks on end several times during the life of that good old trap.

10. Campfire Set

Here's a good easy-to-make set that capitalizes on the fact that coyotes and most fox, bobcats, etc., are pretty damn smart when it comes to getting along around humans. In this case, the trapper is actually beating these critters at their own game, making use of a situation that smart carnivores have found nonthreatening.

The basis, or heart of the set, is a dying campfire. It's important that the fire be smallish and pretty well dead. A hot, cheery coal fire will take all the temper out of an expensive trap, so it's important that care be taken on this point.

I originally got the idea for the set when I noticed that skunks, coons, and coyotes were working our campfires for bits and pieces of food. At the time, I had a fall job wrangling horses and mules for an outfitter working the lower Uintas in Utah.

It was good elk area. The guy's customers were consistently filling about 60 percent of their tags. When they dropped an elk or deer, my job was to take some of the stock and retrieve the meat.

In that capacity, I got around on almost a rotational basis to all of the temporary camps several times each fall. Breaking camp always followed a set pattern. We got up early, saddled and loaded the stock, ate breakfast, stowed the coffeepot and skillet, and took off. Since we were always in

Smart, old trapwise critters can often be caught in a campfire set. The bait seems natural and apparently can be smelled at great distance by carnivores. Human smells are either masked, killed, or occur in a context that does not frighten the animal.

a hurry and moving out to a main camp, any scraps of food or other leftovers went into the fire.

Later when I did come back, I noticed that the campfire was almost always scattered around and dug up. Animals aren't any more afraid of fire than humans are. As soon as the coals cooled, they checked it out.

My first attempt to make a set out of the situation really wet my whistle. There is nothing like the magic of success to keep a trapper's interest revved up. I took a good, new Number 3 jump trap and scooped a hole just big enough to hold the trap in the center of the still-hot smoldering fire. Then I dug down three more scoopsful with the military trenching tool we kept around camp so that I had a place to hide the drag. For a drag, I used a head-size granite rock.

The reason for choosing a Number 3 jump trap was that that was all we had around. Looking back at what happened to that set, it's good to make that point clear.

I scooped the dying coals back around the trap and threw the remains of some pancakes and chili we had for breakfast into the fire. By 7:30 a.m. we were on the trail.

A few days later, we changed hunters. I hauled the party that was leaving along with their meat and gear down out of the hills, and picked up the new group heading out to start their hunt.

The new guys were from Salt Lake and had hunted in the area with my boss a number of times before. About two-thirds of the way back to camp I left them and cut over a little saddle to the east to look at the trap. It was about 11:30 in the morning and only an hour's ride at most out of the way.

The Number 3 jump trap in the campfire was gone. Something had come in and stirred the fire up, but it looked to

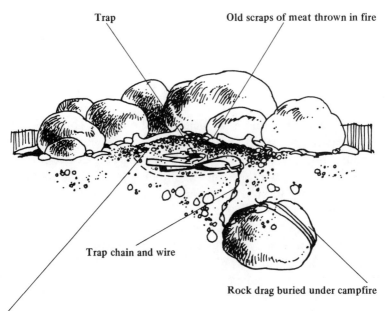

Trap   Old scraps of meat thrown in fire

Trap chain and wire

Rock drag buried under campfire

Dying coals; make sure fire is getting cold or it will take the temper out of the trap and wire.

me as though the burnt food was taken after the trap had been removed. It was something of a mystery. I knew a coon couldn't get past the edge of the clearing with that big trap hooked to a rock on its foot. Even a big, old coyote shouldn't have gotten very far.

I started tracking the drag marks. In some places they were pretty damn faint. It was slow going. Before I knew it, my watch said 1:45 and I still didn't know what I had.

I followed the track down a small powdery trail till it passed a wet spot. Most of the year, a little spring ran through at that point. During the dry time in the fall, the ground was just a little swampy, especially where the horses churned everything up when they went through. There were two or three perfect prints in the muck. It was obvious I had nabbed a small yearling bear.

Slowly, steadily I worked the track. Another hour went by. I wasn't really worried because I was still less than a mile from the horses. The track wasn't looking much fresher. Here and there a rotten log was scattered, some ferns were raked over, or there was a skitch mark in the piney under-layer.

By 4:00 I was worried. By 5:00 I was no longer worried. I was resigned. At twilight, I broke off the chase and hoofed it back to the horses. They were more anxious to get back to camp than I. In forty-five minutes I was drinking hot coffee and eating biscuits.

We never did find that bear. By the time I got back, the drag marks were all gone. After the snow came, I looked around but never found a single bear track, big or little.

Later in the winter after we shut the hunting camp down, I put out a couple of campfire sets around my cabin. They worked quite well for coyotes.

Apparently the critters think that the human smells around camp are perfectly natural and nonthreatening. Any iron smell from the trap is either killed by the heat or is of no concern to even very smart coyotes. They, as well as skunks, fox, marten, opossums, and even the occasional mink come right in and start digging around.

I have used just about everything as bait in the fire. The

best is definitely meat scraps of some sort. Chicken wings are OK. Another good one is cracklings or bacon fat. I have even thrown grouse guts in the fire and they worked fine. Vegetables like potatoes, corn, rice, and beans don't by themselves seem to do much.

About the biggest problem in the West and Southwest is that magpies often get in the set before the critters get a chance to get there. Otherwise, the set is a good idea that I have successfully used from Florida to Washington State.

11. Riffle Fish Set

This set is dedicated to people like myself who think that, as a general rule, simplicity is better. The plan is a model of simplicity. As part of its attraction, the riffle fish trap is the best all-weather stream-catching tool I know. Freezing snow can stop it, but not unless there is a hell of a lot of it.

The best user of a riffle fish set is an otter. Not too many people have otters kicking around their trap lines. Second best is pretty good, too; mink really like this set. Coons will get in these traps in early fall, but are not the least bit interested in getting their feet wet later in the year when it is really cold.

Down South and in most southwestern parts of the U.S., having a frost-free set in one's trapping repertoire is not nearly so important as it is in the north. Most southern trappers can keep their conventional sets functioning virtually every day of the year.

Southern coons will come to a riffle fish set readily if it's possible to find a place to put the set in. It has been my experience, however, that most southern creeks are not suitable for this kind of setup.

The riffle fish set is a bait set. It requires that the trapper have access to a number of four- to six-cm. shiner-type fry fish. These minnows don't have to be fresh, but they have to look fresh.

There are two ways that I get around the fresh-fish requirement. During the winter, I keep my minnow trap set in hopes of picking up an occasional small trout or chub. I also freeze a couple of dozen fish in early fall when it's easier to net or trap them. I have never been able to make a fake fish, or one of those pickled minnows out of a jar, work.

A fish, when put out in the set, has to look like a real fish swimming in the water. Down South where the water in winter is still pretty warm, even a fresh fish will only last about five days. Up North, a frozen fish will stay nicely preserved in the icy water and look good for weeks on end if the critters leave it alone that long.

Basically the idea is to hang a small fish in a fairly fast-flowing, 10- to 15-cm. deep ripple in such a way that it will look like it swam there all by itself. There is a bit of skill involved, but not very much. Obviously the set is made while standing in the water.

Place the fish in water moving fast enough not to freeze in a spot where a fish is generally likely to hang out if it were left to its own devices. I like to place the fish in the lee of a rock or in a depression in a small ripple. Hold the fish in place with a small piece of light monofilament line. Depending on how the water flows, either throw a big loop over a rock or anchor the two ends of the string off to the sides on separate rocks or sticks poked in the creek bed. Don't worry if the fish is a bit deeper than 5 cm. Deeper is better than shallower if the deeper water will stay unfrozen. Of course, the string must be tight and invisible.

Lots of trappers make the mistake of using too big a fish and then anchoring it in shallow, open ripples where they can easily see it themselves. I guess they reason that if they can see the fish, then the mink will be able to see it as well. On the average, I truly believe that mink can spot fish in the ripples ten times better than the most hawk-eyed trapper. Put the minnow where it would logically be and let the mink find it.

The set requires two traps and even then the bait will still

Small streams with riffles are best for this set, but the trapper must plan ahead and store a supply of fish.

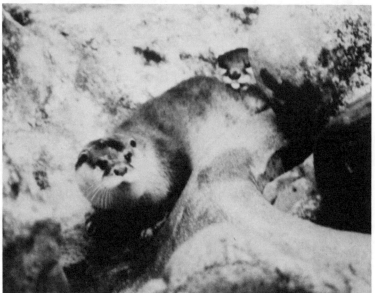

Hanging a small fish on a string near a trap in a stream will bring in tough, smart critters like these otters. The riffle fish set is one of the best cold weather water sets I know of.

be taken half the time without either trap being thrown. Put the traps on either side of the fish. If otters travel the stream, place the traps about 12 cm. from the fish. For mink, keep them in a bit closer to the bait.

I don't know how to keep the bait from being stolen such a high percentage of the time. Perhaps at times, it simply washes away. If there are readers who are using this set and have figured this last business out, I would be glad to hear from them.

The only way to tie down a ripple fish trap is with a drag. Stakes are much too obvious and often can't be put in because the stream bed is too gravelly or too soft and muddy. The creative use of an old log or snag for a drag is always possible. I have made sets with knarled old branches that have steered a critter right into the trap.

A couple of times I have pinched a big old mink in the dead of winter that has dived under the ice to get away. This occurs when the ice freezes right up to the ripples and leaves just a small spot of open water. Signs in the snow always tell the tale as to what happened.

Retrieving the critter—even knowing where it went—is a different matter. If it gets several meters under snow-covered ice where it can't be seen, it's virtually impossible to know how or where to chop. Through the years I have lost several traps this way. A few turn up in spring. Sometimes they are gone forever.

As I mentioned earlier, the set will work in the South wherever there are fast-moving streams. I found a few places to make sets around Crossville, Tennessee, up on the plateau. Down around Tifton, Georgia, the water moves too slow and the stream bottoms are too muddy. It is similarly hopeless south of Phoenix in the Red Rock and Eloy areas. The Santa Cruz and its tributaries are just too unpredictable. North of there in Idaho, Washington, and Montana, the set is very effective.

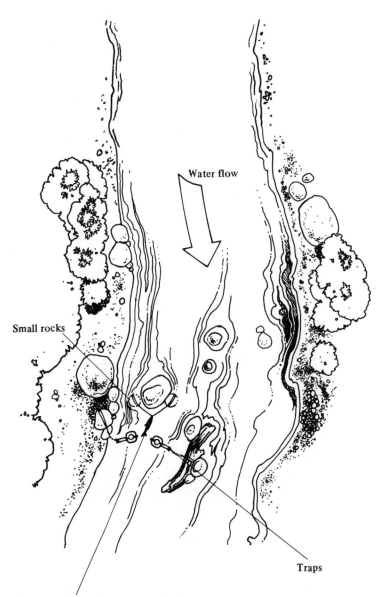

Water flow

Small rocks

Traps

Small fish with a light line through its nose

PART 2

A Few Others That Are Damn Good

Almost every land set requires the skills necessary to hide a trap in a
dirt-hole set. The set is basic and one that should be mastered by almost
every trapper. A few years back, this huge old coyote brought $55.

12. Dirt-Hole Set

Any really useful book on trapping has got to include something about dirt-hole sets. Dirt-hole sets aren't new or unusual, nor, under many circumstances, are they the best type of trap to use. They do, however, have one trait that sets them apart. In concept they are basic—both for a wide range of country and for a large number of different animals. Trappers who learn how to "set a trap into" a dirt hole know how to hide one under virtually any other circumstance.

The same fundamental dirt-hole technique works for fox in Florida, opossums in Tennessee, civets in Texas, and badgers in Oregon. I believe that a variation of the dirt-hole set is even used in Alaska, but never having lived there in fall or winter, I don't know that first-hand.

There is really only one reason the set works as well as it does. And it isn't because dirt-hole sets are easy to make. They are actually quite difficult to put in properly. Nor is it because the sets keep on working when the weather gets cold, snowy, and wet. Tales of trappers who have found fox or coyote tracks over the top of two out of five of their traps the morning after a good solid cold snap are legion.

The only reason a dirt-hole set works is because it duplicates the normal food-gathering habits of North American carnivores and omnivores. The set mimics the food catching and burying techniques used by everything from skunks to coons, bears, fox, coyotes, and even weasels and mink. Resident furbearers are familiar with what they see and smell when a dirt-hole set turns up in their territory. Almost certainly the concept of the free meal also comes into play here. Probably, the fox doesn't know or care who stashed the chunk of pheasant guts back along the old wagon road. All he can think about is the free meal he is about to make off with. Hope that that's all he thinks about until the trap is safely in place, providing the trap hasn't frozen up, the critter doesn't get a whiff of human scent, rain hasn't uncovered the trap, or our fox fails to remember he lost three toes in a similar deal about this time last winter.

Marsh and river trappers don't usually use or even need dirt-hole sets. On the other hand, virtually all seasoned upland trappers will agree that dirt-hole sets are important. They will also agree that making them correctly is tough. A lot of attention must be paid to detail.

It isn't my intent in this case to write a book that will be controversial or generate a lot of antagonistic mail. Yet I am going to list step-by-step directions detailing how I make a dirt-hole set, realizing full well that other trappers might do it a bit differently. In that regard, I will be happy to hear from trappers in Texas, Wisconsin, and even Oklahoma. I promise to be impressed with the new wrinkle you have developed if you will be similarly impressed with the fact that I am too old to change very much.

For starters, I like jump traps in my dirt-hole sets. Jump traps are small and easy to hide. They also are a hell of a lot less trouble to pack around than most other traps. That is something to consider when it might be a kilometer between traps and you are planning on walking and/or driving all day to check twelve to fifteen traps.

Traps used in up-country, dry-land sets have got to be treated; otherwise, they smell too much like humans and steel. I boil my traps for three days every spring in a washtub full of water and about three kilos of hashed-up tree bark. The bark should be from local trees, but try to select varieties that have lots of tannic acid so the trap will color nicely. Cedar and willow work nicely in the West. Oak and

This boy learned to make a basic dirt-hole set. It took three or four years of practice before he was catching a fair number of coyotes.

walnut are my choices in the East. Finish the traps by floating a mixture of one-half bees-wax mixed with one-half paraffin on the boiling water and then pulling the hot trap through the wax. In this way, the steel is blued thinly and coated with wax in one operation.

I guess people who don't have barns hang their traps in a tree in the backyard till it's time to use them in the fall. Having almost always had a barn, I don't really know for sure. The important thing is to keep the traps away from gasoline, oil, and common people smells, as much as possible.

The only pack I have ever found that was worth its salt for trappers is a pack basket. A pack basket carries sharp objects nicely and will stand up on its own, making working out of it much easier than anything else I know of. As with the traps, store the pack basket away from things that will contaminate it when it is not being used.

For tools I use a small steel trowel, three-quarter length ax, pliers, and scraper. The scraper and trowel are standard garden-store issue. Some good trappers also carry along a small mesh hardware cloth sieve. They use it to sift dirt over the trap and "dust" the set. I try to set my traps someplace where it is dry; for example, under a tree or beneath an old stump. As a result, a sieve isn't terribly important. I seldom haul one along anymore. Instead, I sprinkle the dirt off the trowel and make do that way.

Some trappers make dirt-hole sets without a ground cloth. This is, as far as I am concerned, stupid. Some kind of material on which to kneel and work and on which to set the pack basket is absolutely essential. Otherwise, the set will smell so much of humans, it will take weeks before anything will come to it.

The best material for this purpose is a piece of old raw deerskin. I take a whole skin and break the fibers down a bit by pulling it over a log and/or beating it with a maul. Even so, the skin is often stiff and clumsy. Tanned deerskin smells too much like civilization to use as a ground cloth.

Some trappers use a piece of cotton tarpaulin. I think that's a mistake as well. Tarps are impregnated with preserv-

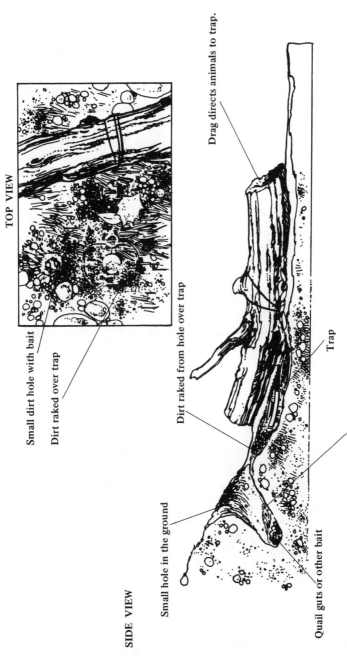

TOP VIEW

Small dirt hole with bait

Dirt raked over trap

SIDE VIEW

Small hole in the ground

Dirt raked from hole over trap

Drag directs animals to trap.

Trap

Quail guts or other bait

Light dirt and chaff covering

ing oils that I am sure the critters can smell even after the cloth is a hundred years old. Sometimes when I get especially disgusted trying to make a piece of deerskin lie down and cooperate, I will switch and use a couple of burlap bags. One is too thin and two are a pain in the neck, but that's the trapping business summarized in a nutshell.

Putting in the trap takes time. My Uncle Dugan used to figure from three to five dirt-hole sets was an awfully good day's work. Wearing rubber boots, walk up to the set location. Pull out the ground cloth. Spread it out, step on it immediately, and put the pack basket on it. Don't move off the cloth until you are ready to leave the set completely. Good trappers don't smoke or spit while making the set.

Dig the hole for the bait down about 20 to 25 cm., pulling the dirt down in a V-shape in front of the hole. Next, dig out a hollow place for the trap about 15 cm. from the hole under the loose dirt. Pile the excess material on the tarp. Set the trap and place it in the hollow. The trap should be set down deep enough so that the pan just clears ground level. I always use a drag rather than a stake to secure the trap. A good solid log or stone that will hold a wire wrap is far superior to a stake, in my opinion.

The wire I like to use is Number 16 black, for those who don't already have a preference. Copper or brass wire is more pliable but is harder to hide because of the color. Always double wrap the wire in such a way that if one strand breaks the other will continue to hold. It is also very important to tie the wire so that both strands take the strain simultaneously.

Use your ax to carefully chop a line down into the dirt, duff, and sand to hide the trap chain and wire. Push the chain in the cleft with your trowel and then close up the cut by thumping it with the hammer side of the ax. In this way, the drag can be kept far enough from the trap as not to interfere with the trap's operation. Ideally, it can be placed to guide or funnel the critter into the trap rather than obstruct it.

There are two methods that I commonly use to cover the trap. In the first, use a large maple or linden leaf to cover the entire trap. Then sift some fine dirt from the trowel over the trap and then, using the scraper, pull the dirt from the bait hole down over the trap.

The second method entails crumpling up some firm leaves or milkweed seeds and putting them under the pan. A ball of fuzzy, loose material keeps the dirt from packing and, theoretically at least, allows the trap to spring on schedule.

Either way, be sure to cover the trap as lightly as possible and only enough to hide the trap. Don't use plastic bags, newspaper, cotton, or other human-smelling coverings.

Take a small piece of quail guts or rabbit skin and put it in the bottom of the hole. Or, as I suggested in the bait section of this book, use a piece of something that is native to the area and keep the offering small. Cover lightly with a centimeter or two of dirt. If there are many magpies around, it will take a bit more dirt to hide the bait. Rake the dirt from the bait hole down over the trap so it looks like the critter made the dirt pile while stashing the bait.

Sometimes if I have it, I sprinkle a few drops of coyote or fox urine on the set. After all these years, I am still not 100 percent sure it does that much good, especially if there are some mink or coons around that might otherwise stumble into the set.

When all is finished, put the tools back in the basket and sling the pack up. Step off the ground cloth and carry it along with any excess dirt left from the set at least 100 meters away. I usually wait three days before checking the trap and then I only walk close enough to be sure it is still functional.

The success of dirt-hole sets is very much dependent on location. One that I put in an apple orchard a few years back, for instance, caught three coyotes, one each night, three nights in a row! Other times I have had traps out six or eight months that didn't even attract a skunk.

One of the advantages of using a drag to anchor the trap is that the critter will pull the trap away from the set and not tear it up. The set in the apple orchard stayed in good condition, even after the third coyote. But other than one coon, thirty or forty days later at the end of the season, I never got another critter. Every night, the coyotes came back and very skillfully stole the bait. I tried everything: using blood, digging the bait in deeper, using two traps, etc. I even tried nailing the bait to the apple tree that stood over the set, but it was no use. The coyotes that survived were apparently so smart they wouldn't put their foot in the trap. For a while I even had trouble finding enough bait to keep the trap going, the critters were gobbling it up so fast.

As it worked out, I sold the three coyote skins for $165. The set was way over the hill about two kilometers from our cabin and took an hour to check. I spent dozens of hours walking to the set to rebait it. As it ended up, I didn't even make wages out of it for the season.

13. Snake Trap

Pointed right down at our feet, the feeble little two-cell flashlight battery barely cut the oppressive, heavy darkness. "Why in God's name didn't we get something more powerful?" I asked. "These lights won't even reach the ceiling."

The echo from my voice bounced around the huge cavernous room like a billiard ball. I knew well enough what I had said but obviously the others in my party were not that certain. Visid, my Thai counterpart, worked his way along the side wall to my right. He answered, but I couldn't tell for sure what he said, either. His heavily accented English and the echoes made the message unintelligible.

Ever so slowly, our party continued on down the large hall over to a set of massive, hangerlike sliding doors. Our plan was to roll the doors back and explore the rooms beyond. As far as we knew, no one had been in this place for at least a couple of years. The interior still looked fairly new, except for the fact that scavengers had stripped out all of the electrical wire. In places, the conduit hung grotesquely from the ceiling.

Perhaps if the lights had been better, I would have been more careful. As it was, we had all we could do just to keep moving. I wanted to blame the shopkeeper in Chaing Mai for selling us the damned unreliable flashlights we were using. But it wasn't his fault. He said we should take the better four-cell kind, but a dollar times six seemed wiser than five dollars time six—out in the broad daylight.

My early-warning radar was on high now, indicating with reasonable certainty that some sort of hell lay ahead. There were six of us. Two corporate officials from a large Bangkok trading company, myself, a processing-plant engineer, and two guards from the bank that now owned the property.

One hundred and fifty centimeters tall at the most, the guards were tough as old leather. They carried 870 Remington 12-gauges cut down to perhaps 65 cm. total length. Brazilian copies of Smith & Wesson pistols protruded from their back pockets. The combination of the huge shotgun boxes, the beat-up pistols, and the brown tattooed little men was imposing.

I speak only very basic street Thai. To make matters worse, these guys were from the Chiang Mai area and only spoke a northern dialect. It wasn't even certain I would detect a warning. Thai is so singsong that it is easy for Europeans to misinterpret even a panicked warning.

Like so much of real life, our original mission wasn't particularly glamorous or exciting. The purpose of our visit was to check out a huge three-factory, vegetable-processing complex built by the Israelis in 1976 near the city of Lam Pun in northern Thailand.

Lam Pun lies about thirty kilometers south of Chiang Mai. The area is rich and fertile beyond belief. At times the farmers grow as many as seven crops a year, including rice, soybeans, corn, beans, melons, squash, onions, potatoes, and other similar vegetables.

Chiang Mai is also the commercial heart of an agricultural industry far more ominous than cereal grains and vegetables. Every year from November through January thousands of hectares of giant poppies are raised in the mountains north and east of Chiang Mai. At maturity, Gin Haw, Karen, and Hmong hill tribe farmers carefully slit the outer layer of the poppy pod, allowing the white latexlike sap to ooze out. The sap in turn is collected and treated to produce raw opium. One hectare of land produces from two to five kilos of raw opium. It all depends on the weather and skill of the farmer.

Shortly after harvest, the hill tribes sell their crop to agents of the drug lords operating in the area. The price depends on supply. Most years, it is about one hundred U.S. dollars per kilo.

The drug dealers send the raw product to their back-country refineries strategically located along the Burmese border. Depending on demand, they produce number two, three, or four heroin. The best—number four—sells for about $6,000 U.S. a kilo on the street in Chiang Mai. In Antwerp or Sidney, it was worth about $40,000 U.S.—that was before the first cutting.

Most people I talked with felt that 60 percent or more of the total world production of heroin came from this area. In the last few years, the Thai government has been somewhat successful convincing the Thais not to raise poppies. However, it is still easy to take a taxi from Chiang Mai out to the poppy fields for those who are so inclined. The fare would not exceed ten U.S. dollars.

As a result of the small amount of harassment the drug lords received from the Thai government, they simply moved their buying stations a few kilometers over the border into Burma. In Burma, new raw opium receiving and refining stations were opened and business went on as usual.

This did not, as I was soon to discover, imply that the drug lords had given up or in any way abrogated their control of the region. They were still there, very active, and willing to spend big bucks maintaining their authority.

Personally, I was in Chiang Mai at the request of American and Australian narcotics control people, the Thai monarchy, Thai business interests, and an American food-processing company. The plan was to bring this unlikely conglomeration of people together to see if the Lam Pun vegetable-processing plant could be restarted.

It was mid Feburary 1982. At that time, the factory had been closed three years. "By restarting this monster," one American official told me, "we can provide markets for alternate crops that the hill tribes raise. Now they rely on opium as their only source of income." In principle, the plan sounded reasonably good. By providing an alternate source of income, the central authorities avoided the politically sensitive situation they referred to as "breaking the people's rice bowl."

"Without an alternate way of making a living, the Thai government simply would not enforce a prohibition against the hill tribes raising poppies," I was told. "If we cut off their income or otherwise harass them, they will raise poppies anyway and will run to either the Burmese, communists, or drug lords for protection," one official told me. No one, however, predicted the intense level of organized opposition the plan would create among the heroin traffickers.

The key component of the mothballed processing plant that I was interested in was the huge freeze tunnel and freezer warehouse. Intuitively I felt that just having the use of these two facilities could cut millions of dollars off the capital cost of the proposed project.

At first we kept the two Thai guards and their ready shotguns ahead of us as we worked our way into the bowels of the plant. Thailand is notorious for the variety and sheer number of snakes one can expect to encounter. The dark cracks and crannies of the plant were, as we all agreed, an ideal place to run into great numbers of them.

The freezer storage warehouses were as black as the inside of a cow. We worked our way into the first large room. Everyone was extremely tense, although the worst seemed behind us. The floor was clean and uncluttered. Not much place for a critter to hide, I thought.

Suddenly, just as it looked like it might be a downhill run from here, the senior member of the Thai business team screamed in panic. It wasn't really a scream, but more of a breathless, traumatic squeak brought on by almost terminal fright.

I crouched and shined my light back to where the frightened old man was standing frozen in terror. The light cut the black just enough to pick up the silvery red iridescent glow of two eyes spiraling in midair not a meter from his head.

Horror of horrors. I realized it was a snake suspended at face level by a piece of cord hanging down from the torn

Some of the old, abandoned buildings at the food-processing plant site in northern Thailand.

These Hmong women are raising giant poppies from which raw opium is collected. Income to the farmers is low, but the Burmese and Thai drug traffickers make out handsomely. The women become addicts from working in the fields.

electrical conduit. The V.C. had, I was told, used this sort of device to protect their tunnels in Vietnam but this was the first time I had ever personally encountered anything like it. "Back off! Back off!" I shouted. The warning didn't do much good. My Thai friend had at that moment forgotten all his English.

Without missing a beat, one of the Thai guards swung around and blasted the hanging reptile. It was a beautifully timed maneuver, except the effect of the discharging 12-gauge shotgun in the room just about flattened us. We couldn't see or hear for several minutes.

After a bit, I flashed my light around. Everyone was looking at the ceiling. Not too far ahead we picked up two more sets of eyes. They were, according to my Thai counterpart, deadly burnt-tail vipers. Apparently, the only reason my friend wasn't nailed in the face or neck was that the people putting out the traps had miscalculated and put the snakes out too early. They were sluggish from hanging so long. The instant the snake brushed the Thai, he ducked. His reaction was apparently quicker than the snake's.

As a result of this experience, I have concluded that, for those who are not afraid to handle poison reptiles, snake booby traps can be very effective. If nothing more, the psychological impact is devastating. Anyone who moves over a predictable path at night could theoretically be put at risk. The emotional-psychological impact even on people who live in the hills is tremendous.

It probably isn't even necessary to hang the snake. Tying one to a stake on a short cord in the middle of a path would be equally deadly—especially if one could make use of a modest amount of ground cover to hide the critter. At night even this requirement would be minimal.

The Thais, Laotians, and Kampucheans I talked with about this incident claimed that this sort of thing is reasonably common in Southeast Asia. In my opinion, the concept and its potential is unnerving. North Americans, especially those raised in cities, would be highly traumatized by such a trap.

Wire threaded through snake's tail and tied to tree or brush.

14. Chicken-Wire Fish Trap

Although not necessarily constructed of chicken wire, this trap design is almost universal. I have seen this sort of outfit used in the Zambezi River by Rhodesians, in Lake Lanau in the southern Philippines by the Moro, in Thailand, Finland, Turkey, and even Australia.

On the other hand, few Americans seem to be aware of this trap or its potential for putting food on the table. When I mentioned it in *Survival Poaching,* I got several angry comments from game wardens who told me the outfit was seldom used anymore. They wished I would have let sleeping dogs lie and not included detailed instructions on how to make the trap.

Basically, a chicken wire, bamboo, reed, or green willow branch fish trap makes use of the principle that an average fish will be attracted to bait in a pen and will swim around the pen till it finds a way inside.

The trapper makes things easy for the fish by baiting the trap with something the fish really likes and, just as important, by making it convenient to get inside the trap.

This getting-inside-the-trap requirement is usually handled by putting a funnel opening in the trap. Theoretically, the fish is supposed to be smart enough to get in the trap but not smart enough to find the small opening to get back out.

In actual practice, I have inadvertently caught several

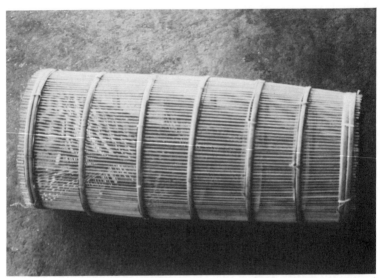

Americans will usually find it is easiest to build a fish trap out of chicken wire. These funnel-type traps are used all over the world. In many places, materials such as the split bamboo shown are easier to find than chicken wire.

The cone opening of this Laotian fish trap lures the prey inside where they find it virtually impossible to escape. The trap is designed and used for fish from 5 to 20 cm. in length.

muskrat in my fish traps. Apparently I have also trapped a nutria or two. The traps were torn to shreds when I got there. Since nutrias were the only animals big enough to tear up the traps and since the area had some resident nutrias, my conclusion is fairly reasonable.

What I don't fully understand is why a mammal that is supposedly a lot smarter than a fish got in the trap in the first place, and why it couldn't find its way back out.

Wire or basket-type fish traps can be made just about any size one desires. I have seen wee models good for smelt as well as huge three-meter-square ocean models that easily caught four-kilogram red snapper, grouper, and mackerel.

In the interests of basic simplicity, I am providing instructions for constructing a trap much like the one I usually use. After that, it will be up to the survivor/trapper to engineer models that suit his or her exact needs.

Any kind of slotted or meshed material that won't melt in water can be used to construct a fish trap. Most people, including every so-called primitive hunting and gathering society I have encountered, use chicken wire if they can get it. Americans can, at least as of this writing, get just about all the chicken wire they want by going down to the local hardware store.

Use the smallest mesh available. Usually that will be half-inch wire. Half-inch wire won't hold minnows with heads smaller than a half-inch, but unless you are a Vietnamese or Filipino used to eating very small fish that won't be a consideration.

Sometimes heavier gauge farm wire is available. It costs more, but it is well worth the added price. The stuff will withstand the beating it must take being hauled in and out of the water much better than garden-variety chicken wire.

I make my traps round. There is no special reason, other than that's the way my uncle taught me to make them, and my uncle was pretty damned crafty about such things.

Most chicken or farm wire comes in either 36- or 48-inch rolls. I like a 125-cm. (or 48-inch) long trap, so try to find wire that width. It saves time-consuming splicing, which is necessary if narrower width wire is used.

Chicken-wire fish traps are ideal for use in small streams where you could spend a lot of time waiting around with a fishing pole trying to catch the limited number of fish.

A 130-cm. trap should have a diameter of about 75 cm. (or 2.5 feet). It isn't written anyplace; I just usually make them that size. Roll the wire into a cylinder and lace it together. I usually reinforce the ends and middle with a hoop of Number 9 wire. It stiffens up the trap and makes it more durable. Put a flat wire-mesh end on the cylinder. The end must also be reinforced with Number 9 wire, and made so it can be opened for baiting to clean out the fish.

The funnel end of the trap is a bit hard to explain to people who have absolutely no idea what a fish trap should look like. The funnel provides a path by which the fish enter the trap. Once in, the fish cannot escape—because the opening is small and because it is guarded by sharp wire ends that jab the fish. Take a look at the drawing of this trap and the funnel's construction should be clear.

Important details to keep in mind are:

1. The funnel should be made of the same size mesh wire as the trap cylinder.

2. The funnel should extend back at least two-thirds of the way into the trap.

3. The funnel should point toward the center of the back of the trap.

4. Last of all, clip off the factory edges of the wire so there are no smooth ends at the small end of the funnel. Be sure the wires all point into the trap so the fish won't get stuck prematurely when entering the trap.

So much for the trap itself. Baiting is another matter. I use fresh pork liver for trout, bass, pike, and bullheads. Cheese attracts carp, bullheads, bluegills, and sunfish. Other baits that have worked for me are chicken guts, doughballs, pieces of fish, calf brains, and even muskrat carcasses.

Sometimes it is necessary to put the more frail, water-soluble baits in cheesecloth bags. Small fish that slip through the wire mesh, as well as crayfish, will quickly devastate these baits if you don't protect them. On the other hand, I have nailed some big bass that I am sure came into the trap to slurp up the crayfish working the bait.

Another excellent bait that I have only recently started using is canned dog or cat food. Leave the food in the can,

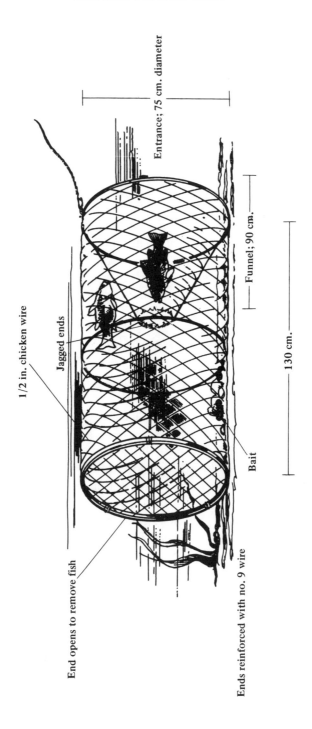

Entrance; 75 cm. diameter

Funnel; 90 cm.

130 cm.

1/2 in. chicken wire

Jagged ends

Bait

End opens to remove fish

Ends reinforced with no. 9 wire

but punch holes in it with a nail or beer can opener. Then place the whole can in the trap.

Often when we were kids, we set our fish traps by simply throwing them in a deep hole in the river without a line or wire to the bank. Thus there was no wire to give away the trap's location. We pulled our traps out with a long-handled garden rake specially rigged for that sort of thing.

One day, I found someone else's fish trap set in our bayou. I raised it up and started the long trek home. About halfway back, I ran into one of my brothers with a fishing pole and some hooks. Earlier that morning he found a nice little school of smallmouth bass in one of the deep holes along the creek.

Smallmouth fishing that early June morning in the hole my brother discovered was probably the best I have ever experienced in my life. We took turns catching fresh crayfish for bait and sharing the single pole. By being very sneaky we were able to drop the line right under the bank. The crayfish swam down to the bottom and were immediately gobbled up by the bass.

Each succeeding fish we caught got a bit bigger. By noon we had about a dozen. The last one weighed four and a half pounds, which is a mighty damn big smallmouth. The belly on a bass that size hangs down grotesquely. To keep the fish fresh, we put them in my new-found fish trap and sunk it in the creek. It was a convenient way of keeping them alive.

It took the two of us to carry the trap with the fish home at noon. We were really proud of ourselves. Smallmouths just aren't that easy to catch. Even including trapping, it was the most bass I had or have ever seen in one place in my life.

Dad saw us coming up the lane and came out to have a look. "Will you look at that," he hollered in astonishment. "Now that is a real trap full of fish."

And so it was. No matter what we said or did, no one ever truly believed we got those fish the hard way. Not that it really matters. They made good eating and that, for the Bensons, was the bottom line.

15. Large-Bait Sets

Usually I won't, if I have a choice, ride a gelding in the mountains. Gelded horses remind me of a lot of American men after they pass forty. They get fat and lazy and have trouble keeping their minds on anything except eating and sleeping. If they had TV for geldings, they would probably watch forty hours a week.

Trailing horses through the mountains in the western U.S. can be damn dangerous business. As recently as eleven years ago, I knew a packer whose lead horse slipped off the trail, dragging nine mules to their death. Mountain horses have to be experienced and alert.

The big red horse I was riding wasn't ideal, but I figured it might be OK. It had been cut at the age of six, after being used as a stud for a couple of years. The horse seemed fairly alert.

Two of us were checking out an area about thirty kilometers from the main camp. This entailed traversing the end of a steep glacier valley.

I suspect that the horses scented a bear, but to this day I don't know for sure. At any rate, the horses picked just about the worst time imaginable to start getting jumpy. The trail was less than a meter wide and dropped off like a thirty-eight-story building. My big red critter laid back its ears, rolled its eyes, and tossed its head.

Several years later, I took some dudes over to the place where I lost my big red mountain horse. The critters had worn a trail to the place my horse had come to rest. Apparently, they were still coming by now and then to look around.

It bucked once, caught itself uphill with its front feet, hung there a minute, and then slid off the narrow trail. Both rear legs went simultaneously. The trail was so steep there wasn't anything but daylight for the next ten meters. I fell with the horse backward.

It landed on both rear feet and hung there in suspended animation for maybe two seconds. A quarter of a second after I bailed out, old red pitched backward one last time and went sailing down the hill.

We retrieved the saddle and bridle, along with my scabbard, rifle, and day pack. Everything was OK except my rifle and camera. They were both totaled.

It was no less than a 200-meter trek virtually straight uphill after we got the gear. Then there was the little matter of the thirty-kilometer walk back to camp. Actually it wasn't that bad; my buddy and I took turns riding and walking.

One of the really good places to put a trap or two is around a large dead critter. In Africa we tracked lions around the carcasses of the elephants we shot. I even built a blind

This little bear came to check out a large dead steer bait. The hunter shot it, but we could just as easily set a trap.

and tried to bag a leopard, but the smell of the dead elephant was so bad we couldn't stand to get near, much less sit for three or four hours. Back on the farm, I used to set traps next to dead calves in the hope of getting a fox or skunk.

I threw several snares in my saddle bags in hope of getting back to the dead horse at some point. Snares are a bit better, in my opinion, than steel traps under these circumstances. Clouds of magpies and even vultures and ravens often get in steel traps faster than you can reset them. Birds don't bother snares much, making life a lot simpler for the poor old trapper.

A couple of days later I got my wish and was able to set out three snares in the trails around the horse carcass. The best place was on the trail above the bait. Predators like to approach a carcass from above to check it out before coming closer.

As I remember, I picked up three or four coyotes in the next four weeks till we shut the hunting camp down. It was an especially good deal because I would bring the coyotes to camp to skin and invariably one of the dudes would buy one off me for twice what it was worth.

The secret to using large baits is to wait a few days till the critters start coming in. Then set the traps back away on the trails leading to the bait. This bit of advice is important. Set the trap too close and the birds and small animals will spring it. Set it too far away, and the critters will concentrate on being careful rather than getting a bite of horse or whatever.

Depending on the amount of cover, I suggest setting the traps from three to ten meters back from the bait. Look for small, natural trails. If there are no trails, try to determine how the animals are approaching the bait and set the trap there.

Three or more traps are not too many to have around a large bait. And three months or more is not too long to leave the traps out. Animals will keep coming even after the bait is nothing but a greasy spot on the ground.

About the only thing that will discourage the critters is if a lot of human scent gets mixed in with blood and other signs

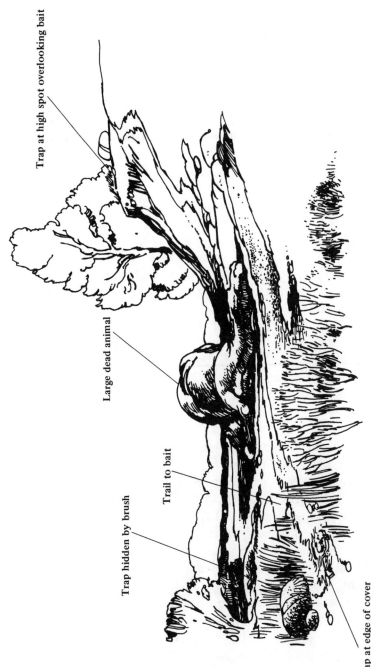

Trap at high spot overlooking bait

Large dead animal

Trail to bait

Trap hidden by brush

Trap at edge of cover

indicate that the area is dangerous for coyotes, fox, badgers, and bobcats. Skunks, coons, mink, opossums, gray fox, and other similar animals don't seem to be put off, no matter what happens.

It is also essential that the trap be set properly. Don't just throw it on the top of the ground. All it will catch are birds and skunks.

Sometimes it is possible to move a large bait and place it to the best advantage. Of course you will have to put the carcass in a place that your vehicle can negotiate. Just keep the animals in mind. They like some nearby cover and/or high ground from which they can survey the bait.

The bait does not necessarily have to be protein. Six or eight years ago I borrowed a hay rake and piled up a bunch of fallen apples from an orchard in the Gallatin Valley in Montana. It wasn't long before a black bear started working the pile. I called a doctor friend who had a pack of pretty good hounds. He liked to run dogs but was not in good enough condition to follow them. I don't know what his patients did, but Doc always came right over when I called. He knew I usually had a good trail and would keep track of his dogs for him.

His strike dog went crazy the minute it got to the apple pile. We immediately turned the other hounds loose. They ran the bear for maybe two hours and then treed it. The bear was average size. Maybe about 125 kilograms or so. It was way up in a tall fir tree.

There were four of us: Doc, myself, and two dudes Doc brought along to watch. One of the dudes had a 30-06 bolt rifle. We discussed the situation a bit and decided to let the dude blast the bear out of the tree. He had never shot a bear and was keen to do the deed. He stepped up to the plate and cut loose. As we determined later, the shot was a good one, right up through the middle of the bear.

It sounded like a glob of fat smacking the parkway from ten stories up when the bear hit the ground. Being a fall bear, the analogy is probably pretty good. Instead of dying, however, the bear hit the ground running. It zoomed right past my left side and grabbed one of the dogs right over the small of the back.

It certainly isn't the best pistol any longer, but for the last forty years I have carried a Hi-Standard Supermatic .22 caliber pistol. Quickly I unlimbered my pistol and at a range of not over two meters proceeded to pump six or eight rounds into the bear's head.

My efforts weren't much better than the guy with the rifle. They say that after five gin and tonics you become bulletproof. Obviously this bear had had more than that! The .22 didn't seem to faze it even a little bit. In the meantime, it was chewing up one of Doc's prize dogs.

I put my pistol on safe and slid it back into the flap holster. Turning, I found the dude with the rifle not an arm's length away, holding his rifle. "Let me have the gun," I shouted.

Without missing a beat, he passed it over. The empty round was still in the chamber. I quickly bolted in another round and, shooting from the hip, blasted the bear through the front shoulders. That finally settled the issue.

Throughout my life I have seen quite a number of bears killed. Some have even been done in with a .22 single-shot pistol. That's all my uncle carried on his bear-trap line when I was a kid. Yet that old critter we got off the apple pile was the toughest bear I have ever seen.

Snaring deer is an especially good technique for survivors who will not otherwise have the time to engage in sport hunting. Although the method is held in contempt by sport hunters, it is very productive without requiring extensive equipment.

16. Deer Snares

Snaring deer is basically a survivor's game. Although the situation may not involve pure or emergency survival, when the technique is employed it is almost always in some sort of "live off the land" context.

Good hunters do not necessarily make effective survivors. In fact, my experience leads me to believe that a strong emotional predisposition causes the skilled hunter to rely on sport game-taking techniques at a time when doing so could easily undo him. Instead of looking at objectives and how to most easily and quickly accomplish them, the hunter continues to be concerned with procedure. It's a surefire formula for disaster when the going gets rough.

This concern with procedure rather than results causes most outdoorsmen to look at deer snaring as something akin to making dirty movies. Everyone knows someone is doing it, but no one really knows who, where, or necessarily why. At the very best, like deer snaring, making dirty movies is seen as an extremely nefarious activity.

Even under ideal circumstances, sport-hunting techniques will seldom produce a net gain in calories. Hunters will almost always consume more energy bringing in game than they will derive from the game they collect. That is why basic trapping/gathering societies that live off the land have no concept of sport hunting.

I used an old, old Franz Sodia 12-gauge double barrel when I lived in Somalia. The firing mechanism on the right barrel was kaput, but that didn't matter a hell of a lot. All I ever used the gun for was guinea hens.

We were operating out of a tent camp 250 kilometers west of Chisimayo. The country was basically thornbush desert, as flat as a flagstone. The guinea hens we had in the area were called vulturinas, mostly because they had heads that looked like vultures. The word itself is, I believe, Italian. Vulturinas came in all sizes and shapes, no matter what time of the year. At full maturity, they weighed no less than one kilogram and were tougher than old leather.

For several months running, I collected the birds simply by waiting till the critters lined up, running down a path. I held fire till as many heads as possible were in sight and then cut loose with the 12-gauge. My Somali trackers understood and approved of this technique.

Sometimes luck was with us. The pattern would spread just right and I was able to knock over eight or ten birds with the one shot I had. As soon as the birds were down, the trackers, who were all Muslims, ran out and quickly slit the critters' throats. They had to do this, plus say the prayer, before the birds died from the effects of the ground sluicing, or they could not, according to the Koran's teaching, eat the birds.

Back at camp, our cook pounded the breasts into patties, soaked them in a mixture of wine and canned milk, and pan-fried them. As a gourmet item, guinea breasts prepared this way were absolutely world class.

Sometimes instead of running away from us, the guinea fowl flushed and flew off. Usually, that was their salvation. We never pursued them. It was easier to look for another flock.

One day, probably to combat the almost-terminal boredom, I blasted a big vulturina on the wing. It was a beautiful hit. The damn thing exploded and crashed.

I fully suspect that the guinea was surprised. My trackers, however, were thunderstruck. They hit the ground as if the guinea had been hit by a 105 air burst. I still remember their white, rolling eyes peering up out of the dust as the four of them frantically crawled to the edge of the strike zone. Later that day, they started to talk about the incident. At night in camp they even laughed about it a bit.

The most incredible part of all this occurred a couple of days later when the trackers and the camp chef made it a point to stop by my tent to ask what in Allah's name I had in mind shooting that guinea. It was just as impossible to explain to my Somali trackers why I shot that guinea as it is to explain to a hard-nosed American sportsman why I snare deer.

But for survivors who are interested in a really good technique for collecting meat, deer snaring is one of the best. The basic concept involves placing a loop of wire across a game trail in such a way that the deer, or even a moose or elk if such inhabit the country, will lasso itself. There isn't a lot of technique involved, but it isn't a piece of cake, either. There are some things you must know before success can be assured.

Virtually any kind of wire can be used for the snare. Obviously, heavy rigging cable won't work, nor will very light-gauge wire. Otherwise, anything in between can be used as a deer snare in an emergency.

Wild Bill Moreland lived for thirteen years in the Idaho wilderness without ever coming out or even talking to anyone. Most of that time he did not have a firearm of any kind. Instead, he relied on snares made from telephone wire he swiped from the Forest Service to catch his meals. The wire, in this case, was Number 9 galvanized. Most people would reckon this sort of line was too heavy and stiff for snare material. Bill Moreland made do nicely, however.

The best wire, in my opinion, is light, flexible 3/32 or 5/32 airplane cable. Brown rubber-coated appliance wire will also work nicely for deer-sized critters. Even when there is snow on the ground, this wire camouflages easily. Other than considering the necessary flexibility and strength, there isn't much else to say about the wire.

The snare can be improved by wrapping or tying it in a lasso, or the survivor can use small cable clamps to loop the ends. Cable clamps are generally better, but the survivor has to have made up the snares ahead of time, before the actual day of need.

One wrinkle that I think is helpful is to put a clamp or block in the loop line so that the lasso will not close down to less than 20 cm. or so. It is very easy to snare a deer and then have it thrash around so frantically that it will strangle itself. A loop block will help prevent the deer from killing itself.

The cable line can vary in length from about two meters up to six meters or more, depending on how the set is made. I like to "spring load" my snare sets by tying them to a torqued sapling or tree branch. I rig the set so the deer will pull the wire, which is under a light, constant pressure, off a retaining assembly. Take a look at the illustration on page 115 for some ideas on how to set up a snare of this type.

It is fairly common, but probably not necessary, to use a lock on a deer snare. Locks are made from a V-shaped steel angle, with holes slightly larger than the wire diameter drilled through the two arms. Refer again to page 115. Keep in mind that the lock will only work if the V-lock is pointed into the loop.

A snare isn't worth a damn if it's set somewhere a deer will never venture. Finding a good productive location implies at least a basic knowledge of game trails, habits, and movements. Survivors who have time to spend in the brush sharpening their skills will agree that deer invariably leave distinctive, easy-to-read signs of their presence. On the other hand, hundreds of thousands of deer live around millions of people without the latter ever being aware of the former's presence. If possible, the first time the neophyte reader uses deer snares should be in the fall or winter when the ground is covered with snow or the trails are muddy and tracks are easy to read.

The snare is set in the game trail at about the high belt-buckle level. Make the loop the size of a bushel basket or in the range of 60 cm. in diameter. Keep in mind that deer walk through the woods in a head-down, nose-leading posture. They customarily push through brushy obstructions along their trails. This characteristic works to the survivor's advan-

Lock; note that the "V" iron is pointed into the loop.

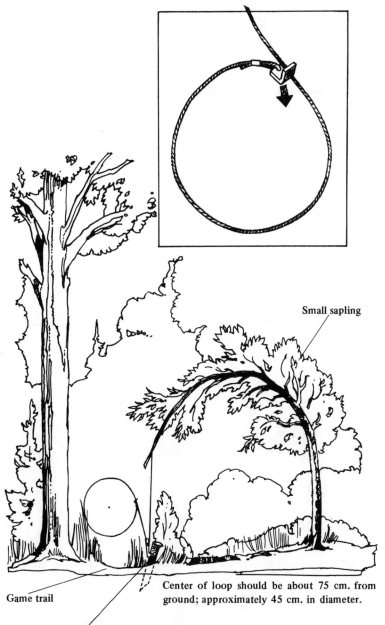

Small sapling

Game trail

Center of loop should be about 75 cm. from ground; approximately 45 cm. in diameter.

Peg in ground trips when pulled, allowing the sapling to put pressure on the snare.

tage. A snare placed in front of a light brush screen will catch the deer as it pushes through the foliage in a head-down posture. By the time the critter realizes it has something more than brush around its neck, it will be too late.

Deer wander around the woods when feeding or if they are spooked off their feeding grounds. Otherwise, they predictably keep to regular trails where they can be nailed with amazing impunity by the astute snare-setter.

17. Quail Recall Pens

Owning and watching a successful quail recall pen is, in my opinion, one of the most interesting and rewarding experiences an outdoor person can have.

Most, if not all, of the traps I have covered in this book are functional tools needed for a tough, lonely, and often dangerous pursuit. Trapping isn't fun. It has its rewards, but about the best one can say for it is that it is interesting and occasionally fascinating. By contrast, a quail recall pen is fascinating but also a lot of fun.

Strictly speaking, a recall isn't a trap. It is more of a cage or pen. But even these terms aren't accurate because the birds spend most of their time outside of the pen. This is what makes the outfit so interesting.

Apparently, hardcore bird-dog trainers still use recall pens. Friends tell me the pens are sometimes available from commercial dog supply houses, although I have never seen them for sale.

Ted Terrel, one of our hired hands, made the first quail pen I ever owned. We saw a picture of one in the *Farm Journal,* and Ted built it. We set it out on the front lawn at the home place. Every afternoon before she started dinner, my wife would turn the birds loose. Then, for dessert we sat on the porch and watched the quail playing around on the grass.

This young coyote, attracted by the quail in my recall pen, snuck in close enough for me to get a picture. Fortunately, my quail were all safe and sound inside the trap.

Someday, if the need ever arises and people tell me I require psychiatric help, I am simply going to save my money and accelerate my recovery by building another recall pen. I have absolutely no question that I could handle anything just by watching a bunch of friendly, cheerful little quail running around.

Except for a few weeks in spring when they pair up to nest, quail are especially social little critters. They like to get together and hunt bugs, eat grass, or just run around and enjoy life. This is what is meant as a "covey."

Once they are part of a core group, quail will go to great lengths to stay together. That is what makes the pen work. All but a few of the birds are turned loose to run around as they please. Very shortly, the released quail will return to their friends who are stuck in the pen. After a couple of hours of trying to coax them out, they apparently give up and run back into the cage for the night. Rather than run off to freedom, they join the few so that they can all stay together. The pen is a trap, but more than that it is a home for the quail—a place they can come back to night after night.

I have had several recall pens. As I remember, the longest I ever kept a covey was for about two-and-a-half years. This isn't bad for a critter whose life expectancy in the wild is about one year. By the end of two-and-a-half years, two-thirds of my birds had either died or not returned to the trap. In some cases, they probably went off to nest. Most likely, some were killed by cats.

There are three essential parts to a recall pen: a holding pen, a partitionable nesting box, and a return funnel. Using good-quality, 2.5 cm. firring strips, build a chicken-wire box about one meter wide and 75 cm. high. Use the smallest meshed wire you can find. Quail are tiny birds and can slip through awfully small holes.

Build in a service door on top of the wire box. It will be useful to feed your charges and clean their water. Leave an opening about 25 cm. square on one end of the box, and groove the wood to accept a sliding door to cover the opening. This door will be used to close off the holding pen from the nesting box.

Using 2.5 by 15 cm. boards, build a solid nesting box that is about half the size of the holding pen. It also must have a sliding door to close it off from the main pen. Construct the box so that it can be securely fastened to the pen, but is easy to separate as the need arises. As with the pen, the nesting box should be fitted with a lid to facilitate cleaning, etc.

The only part left to build is the entrance funnel. Like a lot of these devices, the funnel will be about as clear as an L.A. fog until you look at the drawing on page 121. The purpose of the funnel is to allow the quail to get into the trap but not back out again. Build it out of chicken wire with an entrance about 14 cm. across. Extend it into the trap about 25 cm., finishing off the exit end about 4 to 5 cm. in diameter.

The idea is to provide an opening where the quail can walk into the pen and jump down inside. Place some blocks of wood outside the trap near the funnel to help the birds get up and into the funnel. Because the funnel opening is small enough that the quail have to squeeze in and because it is pointed up in the air, it becomes an effective barrier to the critters inside.

The entire trap should be elevated off the ground about 15 cm. It will keep cleaner that way. Cleanliness is very important to quail. They need fresh, clean food and clean water as well as sparklingly neat living quarters.

Using the pen requires that one have access to a covey of quail. For a pen this size, six to ten quail is about right. I caught my first quail with a net when they came into the corncrib to swipe something to eat. It was a horribly cold, frozen Midwest day, so I don't blame the quail for looking for a handout. I just took advantage of the situation. Most people would find it easier to buy three or four quail from one of the outfits that advertise in the outdoor magazines.

If you use your pen in fall when the birds are moving about, it may even be possible to catch a few additional quail, provided, of course, some sort of quail inhabit your area. Otherwise, it will be necessary to make do with whatever you put in the trap in the first place.

When you approach the pen, you will find that most of your birds will run into the nesting box. Wait till there are only two or three left in the pen and close both doors. Unhook the nesting box from the pen, place it down perhaps 25 meters from the pen, and turn the birds loose.

The birds will fly off about 100 meters and then set down. Dog trainers take advantage of this situation to start their dogs. I just turn the birds loose so they can get some exercise and a good meal. Depending on how wild they are, and how long they have been cooped up together, the released birds

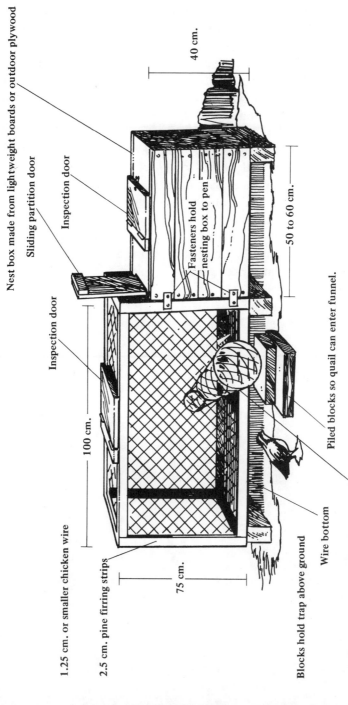

Nest box made from lightweight boards or outdoor plywood

Sliding partition door

Inspection door

Inspection door

1.25 cm. or smaller chicken wire

2.5 cm. pine firring strips

Fasteners hold nesting box to pen

40 cm.

50 to 60 cm.

100 cm.

75 cm.

Blocks hold trap above ground

Wire bottom

Piled blocks so quail can enter funnel.

Funnel extends into cage; large end has about 14 cm. diameter; small end, 4 to 5 cm.

will start whistling to each other in about ten to thirty minutes. Within sixty minutes, the liberated quail will start turning up around the pen. That's when they are interesting to watch. At dusk, they will start running up the funnel into the trap. Sometimes one will stay out overnight. If a cat or fox doesn't get it, it will be back the next day and most likely in the trap by noon.

I found that it was best to position the trap in an open area surrounded by cover. That way you can watch the birds and predators will be less of a problem. However, you will still have to shoot every cat in the neighborhood if you keep the trap very long. A quail pen is like a magnet.

The whole business is loads of fun. I hope more people try recall pens. There is little in life that can compare to sitting on the porch in the evening watching a bunch of happy little quail playing around.

18. What to Avoid: Great Flops

The very first set I ever made in my life was—predictably—a flop! It isn't much of a revelation to admit that the first trap I ever set didn't catch anything. Beginners have to learn. But my first try at trapping was so bad, we still laugh about it today.

One of my brothers had a trap line. He was making some small money from it. I decided to get in the business and trap a few muskrat myself. Old man Reiff told me that muskrat make runs just like common barn rats. Art Gustafson confirmed this when we talked about it at school. Art was in the same grade as I (fifth, I think) but had missed one grade to stay home and help his dad on the farm. Art was, we all admitted, much older and smarter than the rest of us.

That next Saturday after chores, I rummaged around in old man Reiff's barn and found two ancient traps. They were so old and weak I don't think they were even suitable for weasels or barn rats. Of course I should have known better. My brother would have scrounged up any traps worth using.

I went to the creek and looked around. Sure enough, after a bit I found a worn trail down the bank, across the creek, and up the other side. A muskrat run if there ever was one, I told myself. So I set the two traps right out on the open ground where the muskrat could be sure to get in them.

I hardly slept that night. I was so excited. Two muskrat

skins were worth about five dollars. I already had the money spent for a new set of waders. Next morning I ran down to the creek to have a look. My timing was just perfect! I got there just in time to watch 200 shoats running down the bank over my traps and up the other side.

For city people who don't know, shoats are adolescent fattening pigs half of which have been neutered. They are nuttier than hell anyway, and the neutered ones seem to have an even lower I.Q.

My poor traps were trampled so deep in the mud it took me thirty minutes to find them.

Through the years I have tried quite a number of highly regarded sets. Some are regional in nature and just don't work in the areas I was trapping at the time. Others are just plain and simple losers that never have, in my estimation, produced any fur for anybody.

My favorite in this category is the one where the trapper hangs a chicken, grouse, or pheasant wing on a string and puts a trap below it. It's supposed to be dynamite for bobcats, marten, fisher, and fox—the books say. It's an easy set to make, so I tried it often in my early years and, true to form, it was very consistent. I always got nothing!

Perhaps a bad start has prejudiced my judgment, but most run sets fall into this category. Animals usually aren't numerous and consistent enough to run up and down a path often enough to make trapping them there profitable. Unless on the unlikely chance I see quite a lot of tracks and a good natural restriction in the trail, I let that kind of set go.

I have never been able to make a floating-log set work. Baited with sweet corn or carrots, they are supposed to be dynamite for muskrat. I have tried this set in marshes full of muskrat houses, in lakes and bayous, and on rivers in the South. Again the results are consistent. Nothing. To the best of my knowledge, rats don't climb on floating logs, eat carrots or corn, or ever get caught in sets that rely on these traits.

Another set that will usually not work is the one that depends mainly on some kind of weird bait or scent. Don't kid yourself. Turkey gizzards and oil of spearmint are not dynamite on badgers.

Nor have I ever been able to catch coyotes with hamburger and raisins, bobcats and lynx with catnip, or muskrats with cornmeal. One guy even told me he uses old canoe paddles to bait porcupines. Woodsmen who have been around porkies know this last deal at least sounds credible. Only it doesn't work, either!

Generally the more complex a set, the less likely it will work. My rule of thumb is that every part of a set must have a purpose. If everything is reasonable and the set is still complex—my den traps are a good example—count on the set not really working very well for at least six to eight months.

By and large, setting any steel trap in a tree is a mistake. My brother put a Number 1 jump trap in an eighteen-meter buckeye one time. He used an extension ladder to get it right where he wanted it. This is an obviously bad example, but what I am mostly referring to is putting dens in trees. It's hard to hide the trap, and during trapping season the critters don't run up the trees to their dens that often anyway.

Setting a trap at the entrance to a beaver or muskrat den is usually, in my opinion, futile. Often the critter will swim out over the trap, touching it off with its chest. The trap will have some hairs in it, but seldom anything more. If it does snag a critter, it will snag the front leg, inviting a wring off.

Another surefire flop will occur if the trapper puts the bait on the pan of the trap. Perhaps I have been at this business too long, but I can't imagine why anybody would do this. Yet amateur trappers still make sets this way. Perhaps they want to catch the critter by the nose!

Any trapper who has ever just pinched a critter's toe can tell stories about sets that don't work. Undoubtedly, there are more sets that don't work than do. The lesson is to accept the fact that lots of ideas don't produce fur—even if they are simple, well done, and use natural conditions rather than an artificial situation.

My answer has always been to move on to something else. No one ever gets ahead riding losing ponies.